Some Account
of the
10th and 12th Battalions
The Hampshire Regiment
1914—1918

The Naval & Military Press Ltd

Published by
The Naval & Military Press Ltd
5 Riverside, Brambleside, Bellbrook
Industrial Estate, Uckfield, East Sussex,
TN22 1QQ England

Tel: +44 (0) 1825 749494
Fax: +44 (0) 1825 765701

www.naval-military-press.com
www.nmarchive.com

In reprinting in facsimile from the original, any imperfections are inevitably reproduced and the quality may fall short of modern type and cartographic standards.

FOREWORD

WAR OFFICE.

This account will be of great interest to all who served in the 10th and 12th Battalions of The Hampshire Regiment. It is in private diaries such as these, rather than the popular and pornographic pages of the " best sellers," that we re-capture the real atmosphere of campaigning, and learn to understand something of the spirit that made these two battalions play the gallant, uncomplaining and honourable part they did in the Great War. As the Commander under whom these units served in Macedonia, I congratulate Major Cowland on his achievement, and the battalions themselves on the fine record which they have provided for their chronicler.

Geo. F. Milne
X. M.

10 *July*, 1930.

EDITOR'S NOTE

Some time ago I undertook to collect some account of the doings of the 10th and 12th Battalions The Hampshire Regiment in the years 1914 - 18. I have to thank those officers who have given me documents and others who have read through the proofs. It is, I know, a very incomplete account, and if there are other interesting papers forthcoming, it might be possible to issue a further small volume at a future date. I have been at considerable pains to reduce obvious contradictions and errors to a minimum, but have not removed the personal touches in each narrative. I hope those who find any mistakes will write to me.

It is much to be hoped that this volume (which costs 5s.) will reach many of those who would care to have it. Any old member of the 10th or 12th Battalions, if he will state when and where he served with either Battalion, can get it free on applying in writing to me or to Warren and Son Ltd., High Street, Winchester.

W. S. COWLAND.

The College,
 Winchester.
July, 1930.

10TH BATTALION HAMPSHIRE REGIMENT.

IMPORTANT EVENTS AND MOVEMENTS, 1914–1918.

By Captain C. Grellier, m.c.

1915.

Mar. 10.—Left Mullingar and moved to Curragh.
May 3.—Left Curragh 2.30 p.m.
 ,, 4.—Arrived Basingstoke 12.30 p.m.
July 6.—Left Camp at Basingstoke in evening by train.
 ,, 7.—Arrived Liverpool early in morning.
 ,,   Boarded S.S. *Transylvania*, which moved off about 5.30 p.m.
 ,, 11.—Cape St. Vincent sighted 7 a.m., and Gibraltar passed in afternoon.
 ,, 14.—Reached Malta about midday, and Officers and W.O.'s allowed ashore in afternoon till midnight.
 ,, 15.—Left Malta about 6 a.m.
 ,, 17.—Reached Alexandria about 5.30 p.m.
 ,, 19.—Left Alexandria about 5.30 p.m.
 ,, 21.—Arrived Lemnos about noon.
 ,, 22.—Disembarked in morning and bivouacked.
Aug. 5.—Embarked for Gallipoli, which was sighted just before dusk. Weighed anchor about 10.30 p.m. about 200 to 300 yards from shore.
   We landed in small boats and were led into a deep nullah.
 ,, 8.—Moved *via* Shrapnel Valley about 8.30 a.m. to Fisherman's Hut. After dusk moved slowly towards front line.
 ,, 9.—Arrived behind front line at dawn. Moved up to position on left of Australians and New Zealanders.
 ,, 10.—At dawn Turks attacked, and although the attack failed the casualties in the Hampshires were very heavy. Being wounded in the early part of the battle, I have no further particulars of any of the fighting on the Peninsula.
Nov. 15.—I rejoined the Battalion under the Command of Major Scully at Lembet, near Salonika (6 miles). Took train to Doiran.
 ,, 16.—Arrived Doiran about 4 a.m. and bivouacked about 2 miles out of Doiran.
 ,, 18.—Marched to Causli, camping there for the night.
 ,, 19.—Marched to Rabrovo.
 ,, 20.—Marched to Tatarli.
 ,, 28.—Lieut.-Col. Beckett, d.s.o. (then Major), from 1st Battalion, arrived to take over Command.
 ,, 29.—Marched to Kajali and took over trenches from 6th Munsters.
Dec. 6.—Enemy commenced their advance.
 ,, 7.—Enemy attacked at dawn, driving back the Irish Fusiliers who held an advanced post on Rocky Hill. The enemy attacked on the left of the Hampshires' line, and in the afternoon we received orders to withdraw and at night took up a position on Crete Simonet. The night was quiet.

THE 10TH AND 12TH BATTALIONS

Dec. 8.—Just before dawn the Battalion withdrew to a hill behind, leaving one Company with a battalion of the Dublins to hold Crete Simonet. Early in the morning advanced troops of the enemy attempted to attack but were easily repulsed, and the remainder of the day enemy shelled us continually At dusk they attacked in force just as we had received orders to withdraw, and we went back via Tatarli to Dedeli.

„ 11.—Marched back to Doiran.
„ 12.—Took up a position south of Doiran and the village was shortly afterwards occupied by Bulgars.
„ 15.—Marched back to Kilindir Station and entrained for Salonika.
„ 28.—Embarked on H.M.S. *Partridge*.
„ 29.—Disembarked Rendina.
„ 31.—Marched up Rendina Gorge, which is about 5½ miles long.

1916.

Feb. 8.—Marched to Pazarkia.
„ 9.—Marched to Gomanic.
„ 10.—Marched to Ajvasil.
„ 24.—Moved up the Ajvasil Hill to the Azramiri Road below the Hortakoj Mountain.

Mar. 11.—General Sarrail (Commander-in-Chief Salonika Forces) and General Mahon (Commander-in-Chief British Salonika Force) inspected the Battalion.
„ 18.—Moved on to Hortakoj Plateau.

June 4.—Left Hortakoj Camp and marched up the Seres Road.
„ 9.—Camped 5 miles south of Orljak.
„ 21.—Moved to Orljak Bridge, where we formed a defensive line, making a bridgehead.

July 19.—Relieved by 6th Inniskilling Fusiliers, and commenced marching back in direction of Salonika.
„ 22.—Arrived at Adjvatli, where we worked on the Derbend defences.

Aug. 4.—Moved to Dremiglava and camped in the vineyards.
„ 20.—Marched to Kilo. 37, Salonika - Seres Road, where on account of the reduced numbers of the Battalions in the Brigade a Composite Battalion was formed, each battalion of the Brigade being formed into a company, the surplus Officers and N.C.O.'s being sent back to the camp at Dremiglava.
Later the Composite Battalion moved up the Salonika - Seres Road behind the line near Komerjan Bridge.
NOTE.—As I was not with the Composite Battalion, I have no particulars of its movements, but about 7th Sept. they crossed the Struma River and took part in a raid.

Sept. 19.—Reinforcements having arrived at Dremiglava, a company was formed and sent up to join the Hampshire Regiment portion of the Composite Battalion on the Struma River. Battalions were re-formed, but Hampshires consisted of only two Companies.

Oct. 4.—Battle of Karadzakoj Zir and Karadzakoj Bala, in which the Battalion took part, the Bulgars being driven back to the hills behind Seres.
„ 31.—28th Division attacked at Barakli Dzuma, and the 10th Division Prosenik and Patrol Wood about 2000 yards from Kalendra. The 10th Hampshires were in Reserve, but on withdrawal of attacking troops we occupied Kalendra Wood, finding advanced posts along railway.

Nov. 2.—10th Battalion transferred from 29th Brigade, 10th Division, to 82nd Brigade, 27th Division, and we moved to Karadzakoj.
,, 6.—Took over trenches on right of and across Komarjan Bridge.
,, 10.—A half Company relieved Glosters at Ago-Mah.
,, 11.—Two civilians from Seres captured at Ago-Mah.
,, 15.—Battalion re-formed into four Companies.
,, 16.—D Company, who were occupying Ago-Mah, were relieved by Camerons, and marched to Osman Kamilla, to which place remainder of Battalion had marched, also Glosters and D.C.L.I., preparatory to attack on Tumbitza Farm.
At 11 p.m. we moved to Pheasant Wood.
,, 17.—Reached Pheasant Wood about 5 a.m. and dug ourselves in, and D.C.L.I. attacked Tumbitza Farm. We covered retirement of D.C.L.I., and at 9 p.m. retired to Salmah.
,, 18.—Dug in from Salmah to Kakaraska in evening, taking over Glosters' line extending from Salmah to Kispeki.
,, 19.—Glosters moved out to Pheasant Wood and demonstrated in front of Tumbitza Farm while Greeks attacked on right.
We were relieved by 7th Mounted Brigade and moved to rear of Salmah, moving back at dusk to Jenimah.
Dec. 4.—Marched from Jenimah to Beklik Mah to take part with the Greeks in attack on Verhanli Village, The Bluffs and Verhanli Farm.
,, 5.—Greeks drove the Bulgars out of Verhanli Village, and A Company patrol entered the Village.
Glosters and Camerons took Rabbit Wood and Hare Wood.
,, 6.—Moved out of Beklik Wood to within about 800 yards of Verhanli Village. At 11.30 a.m. Greeks attacked village, but were told to cease attack till Tumbitza Farm fell, which in the end failed. At dusk we withdrew to Beklik Mah.
,, 7.—Tumbitza Farm heavily bombarded and Glosters attacked but failed.
,, 8.—Patrol sent to Verhanli Village under Dupree to capture if possible a Bulgar prisoner. Enemy not seen till patrol was withdrawing, when party of Bulgars attempted to cut them off without success. In evening we took over from Greeks the line round Beklik Mah, with one platoon at Arabadzik (between Beklik Mah and Tumbitza).
,, 10.—We withdrew from Beklik Mah about 11 p.m. and marched to Suhabanja.
,, 11.—Arrived Suhabanja 7.15 a.m. and occupied houses.
,, 22.—I left on leave for England.
1917.
Feb. 7.—I returned to Battalion, whose Headquarters were at Ago-Mah.
,, 8.—I joined my Company at Kakaraska.
,, 9.—D Company withdrawn to Jenimah.
,, 13.—The Battalion returned to Suhabanja.
Mar. 16.—We left Suhabanja and marched to Osman Kamilla, where we took over the line from D.C.L.I.
,, 28.—Battalion issued with the new Box Respirator.
May 21.—Relieved after dusk by Scottish Horse, and marched to Ago-Mah.
,, 22.—Left Ago-Mah about 12.15 a.m. and marched via Komarjan Bridge to Karadzakoj, reaching there about 3.20 a.m. We were to proceed to Orljak in evening, but this move was cancelled later.
,, 23.—Returned to Osman Kamilla and took over again from Scottish Horse.

THE 10TH AND 12TH BATTALIONS

June 5.—Cowland (A Company) left Battalion to take over duties of Second in Command of 12th Battalion.
,, 12.—Left Osman Kamilla and marched to Suhabanja.
,, 13.—Reached Suhabanja at 4.30 a.m. Left Suhabanja at 8 p.m., marching through Nigoslav to the hills behind the Struma. I think the Camp was called the "Summer Camp."
About a week previously Bulgars posted a notice in Osman Kamilla to the effect that we were very wise to go back to the Hills to get away from the mosquitoes.
,, 16.—Orders received to be ready to move at midnight to drive out of Osman Kamilla about 50 Bulgars said to be occupying the village, but later message received that Bulgars had left the village.
,, 19.—Bulgars again occupied Osman Kamilla, and we prepared to proceed to drive them out, but they left as before.
,, 22.—B and C Companies took over River Line from Gudeli Bridge to Komarjan Bridge.
,, 24.—A and D Companies moved down to Gudeli, and at midnight crossed river to Osman Kamilla to lie in wait for Bulgars who had constantly visited the village in early hours of the morning.
,, 25.—A and D Companies returned to Summer Camp.
July 2.—A and D Companies relieved B and C Companies in Line, living in mosquito-proof huts, which went by the name of "Meat Safes."
,, 14.—Major Davies, our Second in Command, left to take Command of a battalion in the 26th Division.
,, 18.—A and D Companies relieved in Line by 2nd Glosters, and rejoined Battalion at Summer Camp.
Aug. 6.—Battalion inspected by Divisional Commander.
,, 15.—Capt. Mackay, of Argyll and Sutherland Highlanders, joined as Second in Command.
,, 20.—B and C Companies took over River Line from Glosters.
Sept. 2.—A and D Companies at 6 a.m. raided Osman Kamilla, but found all clear.
,, 4.—A and D Companies relieved B and C Companies.
,, 5.—B Company lay in wait for Bulgars in Osman Kamilla. Bulgars came, but one of B Company's men, shouting out that he saw them, frightened the Bulgars away. They returned a little later and, after a good deal of firing on both sides lasting about half an hour, Bulgars withdrew. Two B Company men were wounded and died later. Bulgar casualties unknown.
,, 12.—General Milne inspected the Line.
,, 23.—Bulgar deserter crossed river and gave himself up.
,, 30.—B and C Companies relieved A and D Companies in Line.
Oct. 3.—Summer Camp demolished, and A and D Companies moved to sub-section H.Q. in rear of River Line to construct a bund to prevent flooding during the winter.
,, 6.—Major Mackay accidentally wounded his hand while climbing over some barbed wire when out shooting, and had to go to hospital.
,, 8.—D Company did reconnaissance at night, visiting Osman Kamilla, Agomah and Dzanimah, Belica Stream near Yeomanry Bridge.

Playford, while cutting piece of wire from Bulgar barbed wire entanglement in front of some trenches, was challenged three times by Bulgar sentry, whom he saw standing in trench.

Oct. 13.—At 8.30 p.m. we marched to Gudeli Bridge and proceeded to Osman Kamilla.

,, 14.—Reached Osman Kamilla about 2.30 a.m.
Camerons and Scottish Horse attacked Homondos, capturing about 150 prisoners. After the show the Battalion held a line to protect attacking forces, on their withdrawal, from a counter-attack.

,, 19.—About 3 a.m. we evacuated the Homondos - Osman Kamilla Line and marched back to Badimal, when Battalion H.Q. and C and D Companies went into billets, A and B Companies being billeted at Apidje.

,, 24/25.—Brigade attempted to get in rear of Salmah and Ada with view to capturing the Bulgar garrisons. The Ada column bumped Bulgar post, being fired on from front and both flanks. Having had orders not to fire, attempt was made to bomb the Bulgars out of trenches. We withdrew, and Glosters attacked Ada from front but found Bulgars had withdrawn. The Salmah column succeeded in capturing about 100 prisoners. There were Companies of the Hampshires in both columns. We returned later to our billets.

,, 30.—Clement and Gibson left Battalion to proceed to India.

Nov. 1.—I was sent to hospital with dysentery.

Dec. 1.—I rejoined the Battalion, which during my absence had marched to extreme right of the line near Tasli. The Battalion had taken over the line from 3rd Bn. K.R.R.C. on 30th November, known as K.C. Line, on top of a high hill. There was another battalion on our right, our left resting on the Drama Road against the river.

,, 4.—Patrol sent out to White Spot Bank just in front of Bulgar line. Bulgars bombed them when close up to bank, but they got back without a casualty.

,, 14.—Patrol sent out to Picket Bank, but found it was not held by Bulgars.

1918.
Jan. 8.—Major Taylor joined Battalion to take over duties of Second in Command.

,, 22.—A platoon went out in front of line to lie up in hope of capturing a Bulgar patrol, but without success.

Feb. 9.—Colonel Beckett accidentally killed by a bomb. Major Taylor took over Command.

,, 15/16.—Relieved in line by Glosters, and Battalion H.Q. and A and D Companies moved back to Bluff Camp near Kato Krosoves, C and B Companies going to Castri.

Mar. 8.—A and D Companies changed places with C and B Companies.

,, 22.—A and D Companies returned to Bluff Camp. B Company and H.Q. were also there, but C Company went to Tasli.

,, 24.—Major Eley, of Suffolk Regiment, joined Battalion to take over duties of Second in Command.

Apr. 30.—The Battalion relieved the Glosters in the Line.

June	15.	—I had to go to hospital with fever. About this time Greek troops took over the Line, and about 23rd June the whole Battalion came back to Stavros later moving across to extreme left of line (Vardar Front).
July	28.	—I rejoined the Battalion, which was split up as follows :—Battalion H.Q. and A and C Companies in Cascades Ravine, just south of Kara Sinanci ; B and D Companies in Pactol Ravine.
August.		During this month we underwent strenuous training for the coming attack on La Table and Mamelon aux Buissons.
,,	31.	—Moved to Parallel 2 just behind front line preparatory for the attack.
Sept.	1.	—Moved into front line trenches at 5 p.m., and at 5.30 went over the top under cover of creeping barrage.

Enemy driven back and we took several prisoners. We had several casualties, including both officers and men.

Enemy counter-attacked during the night, but were repulsed.

We continued to hold line for some time, later moving back to " Locomotive."

I have practically no notes from 1st Sept., but on 21st Sept. big fires visible in Bulgar line, and they blew up a large dump. They had commenced evacuation, but La Mitre was still held by them.

        22.—General advance commenced at about 4 a.m. At 11 a.m., Battalion left " Locomotive " and marched *via* Yatagan Road to Dos de Mulet.

,,   24.—Marched to Negorci.

,,   25.—Battalion formed into two Companies : A and B became Y Company, and C and D became Z Company. Each Company about 85 strong.

,,   26.—Left Negorci at 7 a.m. and marched about 2 miles, halted and moved off again at about 4.30 p.m. and marched to Bogdanci, reaching there at dusk. Camped above the village.

,,   27.—Z Company strength down to 65. Battalion moved to Dedeli.

,,   28.—Battalion formed into one Company on account of very reduced strength.

I was sent to hospital with fever, and have no further information of Battalion's movements.

NARRATIVE 8TH—10TH AUGUST, 1915,
WITH 10TH HAMPSHIRE REGIMENT, GALLIPOLI.

By LIEUT.-COL. W. D. BEWSHER, D.S.O.

August 8th. The Battalion paraded as ordered under G.O.C. 29th Brigade at 10.30 with the 6th Bn. R.I. Rifles : proceeded *via* Shrapnel Gully and Beach Sap to Fisherman's Hut, arriving there at 12.35. Long halt during which a Conference of Officers was held at General Shaw's Divisional Headquarters. I was informed ourselves and R.I. Rifles were attached to his Division and would come under orders of General Baldwin, 38th Brigade. At 1500 hours ordered to follow R.I. Rifles as we were to reinforce attack on Chunuk Bair. As we debouched, our advance was stopped by Divisional Orders owing to heavy shrapnel fire. Resumed march at 1730. Progress very slow owing to crowded traffic in Chailak Dere. At 1930 ordered to bivouac for the night. At 2130 urgent orders to march again. My orders were to follow the R.I. Rifles. Many checks and about midnight long halt, word coming back that the guides had taken wrong road.

August 9th. In the early hours we marched again, following R.I. Rifles, and crossed to Aghyl Dere. By the time we reached there the naval bombardment had commenced. On reaching a point about 600 yards W. of Farm, I was ordered by 38th Brigade to deploy two Companies to take up position on left of R.I. Rifles. This was countermanded almost at once. At this time we were amongst parties of Ghoorkhas. At 9 a.m. I was ordered to fill up the gap on the right of R.I. Rifles and join up with the New Zealand Brigade. I therefore sent A Company and half D Company under Pilleau (Second in Command). B and C in Reserve.

A and D Companies came under heavy shrapnel and rifle fire as they proceeded up the N.W. slopes of Chunuk Bair out of Aghyl Dere. Here I would mention that the N.W. slopes of Chunuk Bair were very exposed and any movement at once brought heavy fire. Major Pilleau (see Message X attached) established the two Companies as directed (along a shallow gully) about 200 yards W. and South of the Farm with his right in touch with the New Zealand Brigade troops. Reinforcements were asked for by the East Lancs Regt. at the Farm. I sent Lieuts. Williams and Grellier with 60 men.

The 38th Brigade Headquarters was close to Battalion Headquarters and I was frequently at Brigade Headquarters receiving verbal instructions. About 1400 General Baldwin ordered me to send more reinforcements to General Johnstone, Commanding New Zealand Brigade. I therefore sent B Company, directing Capt. Hicks to report to New Zealand Brigade Headquarters. Directly afterwards I myself proceeded (*via* our front lines and top of hill) to New Zealand Brigade Headquarters in order to find out for myself the situation on our right. (See Messages A attached.) About 1500 General Johnstone, Commanding New Zealand Brigade, told me it was useless to send him more men and at my request gave me the written message B.M. 866 so that I might shew it to General Baldwin. B Company was returned by O.C. N.Z. to my Headquarters and after a long detour came into my Reserve again.

See Message marked R. About 1800 at 38th Brigade Headquarters I received orders for night dispositions. The general line was pointed out to me by the Staff. At dusk this line was taken up : half A Company (Hellyer and Cheesman) on right. 60 men D Company (Hayes). Half B Company (Hicks and Shone). C Company on left joining up with R.I. Rifles. 1 M.G. with Griffith in front of Battalion Headquarters ; 1 M.G. half-way up hill. I relieved what officers and men I could, including Major Pilleau, Black-Hawkins and Bell. When I visited this line during the night I found Lieut. Griffith wounded beside his gun about 2 a.m. After dusk I found Hayes and his men well posted close to the Maoris (New Zealand Force) on top of hill.

August 10th. At midnight, 9th/10th, the Wilts passed through apparently to take up position with New Zealand force. Bursts of fire all night and at dawn heavy firing. About 4 a.m. I moved my Reserve under Black-Hawkins to the hill behind 38th Brigade Headquarters to avoid shells falling round Battalion Headquarters. About 5 a.m. I noticed parties on top slopes of Chunuk Bair retiring. I proceeded to join the Battalion Reserve under Capt. Black-Hawkins, leaving Major Pilleau and the Adjutant (Faith) at Headquarters. The Reserve was pushed into the firing line. At 6 a.m. I was wounded and taken to a dug-out. After being bandaged up, I again proceeded back towards the front line and was met by the Staff Captain, 38th Brigade, who told me that both Generals Baldwin and Cooper, their Staff and O.C.'s Battalions were either killed or wounded. I therefore assumed command. The Staff Captain reported that the Turks had turned both flanks. I visited the front line and found the line held by men of C Company, some men of North Lancs. Regt., and on the left some R.I. Rifles. I despatched messages asking for reinforcements. About 8.45 a.m. Hicks came in and reported he had been driven back. The Staff Captain reported the Turks had turned the left flank. At 10 a.m. I considered the position untenable and retired the line back to re-form in nullah behind hill, about 300 yards to rear, to be in touch and line with New Zealanders and other troops. I was shortly afterwards sent to Casualty Clearing Station by Lieut.-Col. Burrows, G.S.O.

W. D. BEWSHER,
21 *May*, 1927.

NOTES.

(a) I was informed that after I left Battalion Headquarters Major Pilleau some time later collected all men and made a counter-attack presumably past Griffith's M.G. post.

(b) The distance between 38th Brigade Headquarters and my Battalion Headquarters was only about 200 yards. At the Brigade Headquarters with General Baldwin there was also General Cooper and his Staff. Most orders I received through 38th Brigade, but some came from 29th Brigade Staff.

(c) I would estimate the distance (as the crow flies) between 38th Brigade Headquarters and New Zealand Brigade Headquarters to be about 400 yards, but direct communication was most exposed.

(d) The Right of the 10th Battalion Line on the afternoon and evening of 9th was close to Pt. 270, as when I was there with Hayes at 1300 I could get a view to the W. and N. for miles and I realized how very narrow the top of the hill was. At nightfall I was in the trench held by the Maoris (New Zealand Brigade) close to our right.

(e) I attach Messages A, B, C, D, which may help to show the importance attached to reinforcing the New Zealand Brigade. D gives the position of F. Ambulances.

W. D. B.

P.I. Ninth. X.

To :—Officer Commanding.

On reaching top of gully found old entrenchment made by New Zealanders yesterday and destroyed this morning by fire from our own ships' guns. Halted men at head of ravine and went on to reconnoitre, hoping to occupy abandoned trench and edge of spur towards N.E., but found it commanded by Turkish redoubt on high ridge opposite and any movement attracted heavy machine gun and shrapnel fire. Remained thus until 1 p.m., then tried to move up again, but as soon as men were extended, swept by continual shrapnel, so went back to head of gully where there is some cover. Shrapnel still comes over, but not so bad here. Propose to remain here until dusk and then try and occupy old trench and repair it.

A. L. PILLEAU.

2.20 p.m.   Your message received : am preparing to
Pte. Smith, D Coy.   meet attack.

To :—O.C. Hampshire Regt. A.

Sender's Number, B.M. 866. Day of Month, 9th.

From experience I have found it impossible for troops to move by day beyond the line I am now on (80 K.I.). I have therefore ordered back three separate parties which have arrived here to rejoin Battalion in rear of Farm. aaa. I do not consider it possible for you to reach Chunuk Bair by day.

From N.Z. Inf. Bde.
Place, 80 K.I.
Time, 1510.

A. H. JOHNSTONE, Bde. Genl.
Commdg. N.Z. 2nd Inf. Bde.

To :—O.C. 10th Hampshire Regt.   A.
Sender's Name, Z.B.I. 26. Day of month, Ninth.

Following received from 13th Division. You must hold on to the Farm and whatever ground you have gained on its right with a view to joining up with General Johnstone. aaa. It is imperative that you hold on at all costs. aaa. Lieut. Griffith appears to be well forward of general line. aaa. If so can he be brought back to that line, between ourselves and General Johnstone? aaa. Only to be done if loss will not be incurred. But his situation should be considered to-night.

From :—29th Inf. Brig.
    1430.

To :—G.O.C., 29th Inf. Bde.   B.
Day of Month, 9th.

Hampshire Regt. immediately reinforce General Johnstone's left on spur 81 A 4 and link up with him.

From :—38th Bde.   R. D. BAKER, Capt.,
                                                    Bde. Major.

To :—O.C., 10th Hampshire Regt.   C.
Sender's Number, Z.B.I. 26. Day of month, Ninth.

G.O.C. 38th Inf. Brig. directs you to advance somewhat so as to reach top of spur running from you direct to us.

From :—38th Inf. Bde.
    1325.

To :—O.C., 10th Hamps.   D.
Sender's Number, Z.B.I. 25. Day of Month, 9th.

41st Field Ambulance at junction of Northern and Southern branches of Aghyl Dere. aaa. 40th Field Ambulance in Chailak Dere at the point where we left it last night to cross to Aghyl Dere, *i.e.* just S.W. of Little Table Top.

From :—29th Inf. Bde.
    0844.   A. McCLEVERTY, Capt.

To :—Comdg. Hampshires. R.
Sender's Number, B.M. 1835. Day of Month, 9th.

You will arrange to entrench two Companies of your Regiment to-night as verbally ordered, placing 25 men to protect donga and report to me as soon as completed.   aaa.

R. D. BAKER, Capt.
B.M.

From :—38th Bde.

NARRATIVE 10TH—22ND AUGUST, 1915, WITH 10TH HAMPSHIRE REGIMENT, GALLIPOLI.

By LIEUT.-COL. L. C. MORLEY, C.B.E.

August 10th. The first line reinforcements for the 29th Brigade together with reinforcements for 13th Division, left Lemnos August 9th. The strength of the 1st L.R. for the 29th Brigade was 650 all ranks, those for the 13th Division numbered 400. Major L. C. Morley was in command of the whole Detachment. The reinforcements for the 10th Battalion consisted of Major Morley, Capt. Hudson, 2nd Lieut. Calderwood, and 145 rank and file. The passage across to the Peninsula was made at night (August 9th/10th). A heavy bombardment of Achi Baba was taking place. At 9 p.m. we approached Anzac Cove, our destination. As the ship got close to the landing pier some casualties occurred on board caused by indirect fire from the Turkish position.

The ship anchored about 400 yards from the pier. A launch came alongside and the detachment, 50 at a time, were put ashore. This was completed by 2 a.m., August 10th. All except the 29th Brigade reinforcements were led up a narrow gully facing the pier. The 29th Brigade reinforcements, led by a guide, followed the shore eastwards to the sap that terminates at the Fisherman's Hut. Keeping touch during this march was of extreme difficulty; branch saps kept leading small parties of men astray, although the precaution was taken of posting a man from the advanced party at each one of them. At 5 a.m. on the 10th the party were eventually collected at 13th Division Headquarters. Lying in long lines in front of these Headquarters were the wounded from the battles of the 7th, 8th and 9th. Orders were received from Divisional Headquarters for the reinforcements of the Leinsters and R.I. Rifles to remain at Divisional Headquarters. The Hampshires and Connaughts, guided by an Australian N.C.O., proceeded up Aghyl Dere and at about 4 p.m. reached 39th Brigade Headquarters. 39th Brigade Headquarters was situated on the eastern extremity of a ridge that ran parallel to the Chunuk Bair; a flat-bottomed valley, 500 yards broad, separated the two features. Facing Headquarters and about half-way up the slope of the Chunuk Bair is a building known in the previous battle as "The Farm." A little to the west of the farm was "Dead Man's Gully," which at this period was full of dead; the wounded of both combatants had sought shelter in it during the previous battles and no opportunity was ever afforded of evacuating them.

After the battles of the 7th, 8th and 9th the 29th Brigade ceased to exist as a Brigade. All the personnel of the Brigade Staff, with the exception of one N.C.O. clerk, were casualties. The units of the 29th Brigade, Leinsters excepted, were attached to the 39th Brigade pending re-forming of the 29th. (On my arrival the Leinsters were detached to " No. 5 Section of the Defence " and presumably were attached to an Australian Brigade.) On reporting my arrival at 39th Brigade Headquarters, I was ordered to collect the Hampshires and with the reinforcements to re-form the Battalion and command it. It was a difficult matter to collect the Battalion, as no one seemed to know where the remnants of the Battalion were to be found. Furthermore, the ridge on which Headquarters was situated was the actual front line and was subjected to very heavy fire from all arms. A Turkish counter-attack was momentarily expected. The remnants of the 39th Brigade and 29th Brigade were literally hanging on to the ridge by their eyelids. Added to the confusion and general disorganisation, there was a great lack of water, which added to the general discomfort. Finally I came across a group of 80 Hampshire men under command of Sergt. Lewis, and learnt that Lieut. Hellyer, in command of about 35 men, was holding an underfeature in advance of Brigade Headquarters.

At 6 p.m. the Battalion, all that was ever found, was collected behind Brigade Headquarters and numbered with reinforcements about 280, but owing to the lack of cover, casualties were occurring continuously.

At 7 p.m. I was ordered to take the Battalion back to a little valley some 200 yards from Brigade Headquarters. In this valley was the only available water supply, which consisted of a Turkish well. Both the valley and the well were under continuous machine-gun and rifle fire. Efforts were made during daylight to get water from the well, but such efforts were fruitless, those making the attempt were either killed or wounded. The valley in which the Battalion found itself was a branch depression of the Aghyl Dere and lay on the western side of it. The valley behind Brigade Headquarters was a continuation of it, but lay on the eastern side.

At 8 p.m. orders were received from Brigade to make a sap from Brigade Headquarters to the Turkish well. This was a difficult piece of work to carry out, as the men who had been through the previous battles were quite physically exhausted and the reinforcements themselves had been without sleep for 48 hours.

The Battalion organisation was completed at night and was as follows :—

C.O.	Major Morley.
Q.M. and Adjt.	Lieut. Saunders.
A Coy. ...	Lieut. Hellyer.
B ,, ...	Sergt. Mears.
C ,, ...	Lieut. Hudson.
D ,, ...	2nd Lieut. Calderwood.

There were several men without rifles and equipment and it was several days before deficiencies were made good.

At 10 p.m. orders were received from Brigade Headquarters to find a burial party at once of 1 officer and 100 men. 2nd Lieut. Calderwood left at once with this party. This party had to work between the lines and suffered severe casualties. In the meantime work was commenced on the Sap. At first no tools could be found, but some were eventually borrowed from a battalion of the Liverpool Regiment, who had joined us in the valley. The ground was very rocky and although work was continued throughout the night, progress was very disappointing. Efforts to obtain water were fruitless, the wells under Brigade control having run dry. Eventually Saunders was dispatched to the coast with a party of men and returned on the 11th with sufficient to give each man three-quarters of a pint. Efforts next day to obtain water from the same source were unsuccessful, as there was not sufficient on the coast to supply the wounded and beach parties.

August 11th. All units in this sector, Liverpools, Warwicks, R.I. Rifles, and Hampshires, made efforts to get water from the Turkish well during daylight, as the heat was intense, but no sooner did a party of men make the attempt than it was barraged with shell and machine-gun fire. Continued cleaning up equipment and getting rifles into working order. The Q.M. of the defunct 29th Brigade Staff reported himself to me and informed me that I was the senior officer in the Brigade and asked for instructions. Subsequently Col. Jourdain was found and brought the Q.M.S. to him. Work on the Sap was continued throughout the night, but the Turks having noticed the excavations, kept the area under continuous machine-gun fire throughout the night. All units in this area were put on to the Sap, but progress was very slow owing to the rocky nature of the soil.

August 12th and 13th. Same conditions as for the 11th.

August 14th. At 10 a.m. orders were received for the Battalion to report back to Brigade Headquarters. This was effected by midday. Early in the afternoon the Turks having shelled the reverse slopes of the ridge, one shell alone accounted for five of our men and we lost some 20 altogether. The ridge being rock, the only cover to be obtained was by lying flat against the slope. A burial party sent out the previous night returned with five casualties. Being ordered to report at Brigade Headquarters for orders at 4 p.m., I received instructions that the Battalion was to take over that night the defence of the sector known as Goorkha Trenches. These trenches were on the same ridge as the one we had been sheltering behind, but about three-quarters of a mile further east, *i.e.* towards Suvla. This amounted to an extension of the Brigade front. The reason for this extension was to relieve the

Goorkhas so that they could get some rest. On the left of the trenches was the 16th Australians, and on the right a battalion of the Warwickshire Regiment. Just beyond Goorkha Trenches the ridge makes an abrupt right-angled turn towards the north, thus causing a salient; from the top one looks down into the valley, already mentioned, which lies between it and the Chunuk Bair. Here the latter overlooks us, enabling the enemy to fire down into our trenches. This was especially so of that portion of the Chunuk Bair mass, known as the Abdelrahman Bair, which lay half-left from us and enabled the occupants to enfilade us. The trench itself ran along the top of a little cliff that crowned the ridge, until at the salient, and for a couple of hundred yards around it, there was a sheer drop of 60 feet. At the foot of this ran a newly-constructed first-class Turkish military road, properly graded and embanked, and evidently made before the War; it was somewhat astonishing to see such a perfect military road amid such desolation. From the foot of the salient ran a knife-edged spur towards the junction of the Abdelrahman Bair and Chunuk Bair. Behind the trenches the valley had narrowed to but a few yards in width and sloped up to join the crest of the ridge of the salient. The salient was held by the 16th Australians, but a couple of days after our arrival we took this over from them. The knife-edge spur running from the salient to the Chunuk Bair was held by the Turks, whose trenches here were about 100 yards from ours. The range from Goorkha trenches to the enemy trenches on the Chunuk Bair was 1,400 yards.

August 15th. Conducted by Major Pollock, Brigade Major of the Australian Brigade on our left, I went over by daylight to Goorkha Trenches to make preparations for taking them over that night. This took some time, as the whole area being swept by machine-gun fire, one could only make headway by making rushes between the machine-gun bursts. I got back at dark, had the Battalion fallen in, and at about 2.30 a.m. got the Battalion into the valley behind the trenches. The relief was carried out by 3 a.m. At night it was not realised how shallow Goorkha Trenches were, hardly 2½ feet in places, but daylight showed that cover from frontal fire and enfilade fire could only be obtained by crouching in the trenches. The ridge was of a very hard clay with numerous rocks, and no impression could be made with the entrenching tool. Plans were made for the trenches to be deepened the following night and tools were obtained. Turkish snipers were very active, and we had several casualties not only from this source, but from the fire from the main position. It was two or three days before we got ascendancy in this respect and we had to pay dearly before getting it. The forward slope of the ridge was covered with dead from the previous battles, and at night we sent out burial parties to bury them. In addition to the defences on the ridge there were two "listening posts" in the valley beneath, which could only be entered and left at night.

August 16th. Considerable progress was made in deepening the trenches and constructing communication trenches from the valley behind them. The traverses were increased in height to protect from the enfilade fire from the Abdelrahman Bair. Two machine guns arrived, lent by the Warwickshire Battalion on our right, the Battalion having lost theirs in the previous battle. The strength of the Battalion on this date was 200 ; casualties and sickness had accounted for some 80 since the 11th. The area in which we found ourselves had evidently been the site of a large Turkish encampment which had been hastily abandoned, as the ground was littered with great quantities of Turkish equipment. Half rations only had been issued since August 11th. This was due to the congested state at the base, Anzac Cave, and to the fact that stores could only be landed at night. On moonlight nights it was almost as clear as day and the supply ships could easily be seen and fired at from the Turkish positions.

August 17th. We took over the salient from the 16th Australians. The salient, for some reason, was a source of anxiety to the Turks. It was under machine-gun fire all day, but during the periods of the morning and evening " hates " the intensity of the fire was so great that it was quite impossible to hear oneself shout. The salient had to be held as it dominated the whole ridge, comprising the Brigade front. It could not be entrenched owing to it being almost solid rock. It was therefore protected by a breastwork. Only occasionally did the Turks use artillery against it, but with little effect.

August 18th and 19th. The Battalion remained in the same positions, improving the defences and losing five or six men every day.

August 20th. At 6 p.m. received orders from Brigade Headquarters that the Battalion was to be relieved that night and was to move to an assembly position, a gully, behind and to the left of our present position. It was thought that this meant a rest, which was urgently required by those who had been continuously in action since August 7th, but the concluding sentence of the order was to the effect that " It is essential that the men be given a good night's rest," and this seemed to imply something ominous. Three days previously the remnant of the R.I. Rifles had been sent to us. It consisted of 1 sergeant and 35 men ; this was all that was left of that fine Battalion. I considered them quite unfit for any active work and kept them in reserve. On the day we left Goorkha Trenches they were sent down to the shore. The Battalion was relieved and reached its assembly position at 10 p.m. We were informed that we were transferred to the 39th Brigade, commanded by Brig.-General Russell, but at this time units were so mixed up that it was difficult from day to day to find out in what Brigade the unit was serving. The assembly position of the Battalion was immediately in rear of that point where the

Australian main defence line bent northwards at right-angles to the coast. About three miles away to the east was the spur, which formed the extremity of the Abdelrahman Bair, where that mass turns northward to the sea. Between us and this spur was the Anafarta plain, the coast of which formed Suvla Bay. South-east were the foothills of the Chunuk Bair. One of these features was " Hill 60," which was the objective of to-morrow's battle. In front of us the line was held by Australians and the 6th New Zealand No. 10 Brigade. On this night the men got their first peaceful night. At 11 p.m. orders were received for O.C. Units to meet General Russell at daybreak in the front trenches of the 6th New Zealand No. 10 Brigade.

August 21st. At about 5 a.m. all Unit Commanders were assembled in the place detailed and General Russell gave out his orders for the battle, which were briefly as follows. The Suvla Bay force, whose forward trenches were plainly visible, was to make another attack with the view of gaining ground. The left of the Australian line was to co-operate and bring this line forward and so straighten it out. This would automatically be done by capturing Hill 60. The attack was to be made by the 6th N.Z. No. 10 Bde., Connaught Rangers and Hampshires. The Connaught Rangers had been in reserve during the previous battle and had suffered few casualties and were over 600 strong. The task set the Hampshires was an extremely difficult one. They were to advance behind the 6th N.Z. No. 10 Bde. and then pivot to their right and form a defensive flank covering the right flank. It will be seen the direction of the attack exposed the whole line to enfilade fire from the Turkish main position on the Chunuk and Abdelrahman Bair, and also from the foothills, which in some cases were barely 200 yards distant. The ground to be covered consisted of flat-topped spurs swept by frontal and flank fire.

Half an hour before Zero hour there was to be a bombardment carried out by the destroyers and monitors at sea and by field and mountain artillery on land. The attack was to start at 3.30 p.m. On my return to the Battalion everything was made ready. At midday General Godley, commanding the Corps, accompanied by General Skene, visited the Battalion and wished the men the best of luck. The bombardment started at 2.45 p.m. Owing to the necessity of preserving secrecy there was no previous registration by the artillery. Accordingly the fire from the ships was most ineffective. There is no doubt that the bombardment woke up the Turks to the fact that an attack was pending, and the opinion was that owing to its ineffectiveness, it would have been better for the bombardment to have come down on the Turkish approaches at Zero hour. The Battalion was brought to just behind its " starting line "—the 6th N.Z. No. 10 Bde. trenches—and arrived there at 3.30 p.m. At this hour the 6th N.Z. No. 10 Bde. began to advance, but they were not clear of the starting line until 4.15 p.m. The result of this was that in our section of the attack the long intervals between successive waves caused the attack to lose weight.

The advance to the Turkish front line trenches had to be made first across a gully, then a flat-topped ridge, then another gully, and finally a climb up to the trenches. The Battalion advance was organised into four waves, each consisting of a Company. It was important, in view of orders to form the defensive flank, that we should save casualties and not be drawn into a frontal fight. It was hoped the 6th Mtd. Bde. would capture the Turkish trenches and so allow us to wheel to the right. The leading Companies of the 6th Mtd. Bde. managed to get across the flat-topped ridge with few casualties, but their appearance on it gave the enemy the correct direction of the attack, with the result that the ridge became a perfect inferno, swept by artillery and machine guns from the Turkish main position. The Battalion was brought to the foot of the ridge, where I found 6th Mtd. Bde. H.Q. The O.C. informed me that only a few of his men had been able to get across. On making a reconnaissance from the top of the ridge, I saw that small parties of the N.Z.'s had managed to get into the front line trench and were bombing their way along it. It was obvious that they must be supported and as the 6th Mtd. Bde. had no men available I decided to support them in their attack and trust to have sufficient men subsequently to form the defensive flank. I sent this change of plan back to Brigade Headquarters. Lieut. Hudson led the advance with his Company. Only a few men survived to get across the ridge. He was followed by D Company and then A.

Both the two last Company Commanders were killed while crossing and nearly all their men were casualties. At this period the top of the ridge, covered with short scrub, was set on fire. In advancing over with the Reserve Company (B) I was wounded and directed Saunders, who was acting as Adjutant, to take the Company and any men he could collect back to the gully and endeavour to cross the ridge lower down. This he succeeded in doing, and met Lieut. Hudson. The attack of the Connaught Rangers on the left was successful as far as the first objective, but in no case did the attack anywhere on the front succeed in capturing their final objectives. The battle died away about 6 p.m. The Battalion did not take part in any further fighting. There were over 100 casualties out of its strength of 180 during this battle.

EXTRACTS FROM CAPT. F. M. HICKS' DIARY

Written on Hospital Ship *Neuralia*, 12th and 13th August, 1915.

Sunday, August 8th. In middle of breakfast fell in. Fell out again. Fell in again about 0900. Marched north (Parry hit in thigh by water tanks) over spur under Sphinx down to Ocean Beach. Then through the Great Sap along shore. At rest camp by Fisherman's Hut, between Sazli Bait and Chailak Dere, we and R.I. Rifles halted on sand: a few spent bullets. Got some water. Then waited while Rifles doubled round spur into Chailak Dere: took a long time: I mostly sat by and smoked and watched the shrapnel: very agreeable three hours. Then we got more water and were about to make tea when ordered round into the Dere. So round into the nullah, up it, across some open land (a few bullets) into hollow in the hills. There told to bivouac about 1900. Made some tea and was lying down when ordered to fall in at 2030. Started marching slowly up Chailak Dere; road blocked with mules and with wounded coming down. Halted about every four minutes: by 0500 we had done 1½ miles: fearfully tiring: very thirsty.

Monday, August 9th. About 0500 Staff Officer told me we had been supposed to take part in dawn attack: now we should probably get heavily shelled. We were not. Sun got up. We came into the region of hot, dusty, swollen, brown, stinking corpses lying about everywhere. We marched up nullah, the upper part of Aghyl Dere: good many bullets about. Finally up on to foothills, where our men were mustering to attack ridge. I collected Company and was told to place it on left of C to left of Rifles for attack. Ground (I think part of open ground of the Farm directly below Chunuk Bair) there reported impossible because of machine guns: so we lay and did nothing: few men hit: German hit. Then told to hold B in reserve in a hollow while A and D attacked a hill. So lay under scrub, very tired and thirsty. Sent off 6 and 7 Platoons on fatigue: suddenly ordered with remaining half Company to support A and D: found they had come back hit badly. Reported to C.O.; he told me to "attack that hill at once and entrench on top facing half left." So A and we went for it together. We, on the right, crawled up through scrub: shrapnel pretty thick; in doing so lost direction and got over ridge into New Zealanders' support bivouac. Made men lie down. I wanted to push on to join N.Z. left: but their General (Johnstone) said that was impossible: we should lose 50 per cent., so Major Jackson led us down the valley (Chailak Dere) to show us way across into the main (Aghyl) nullah. On way rested troops and gave them water. They were quite exhausted. Sergeant Major fainted. (Met two New Zealanders bringing in four snipers they had captured: they were leading them off to shoot them. The Turks caught us by the hand and begged for mercy. But we weren't feeling very merciful to snipers just then.) We lost a good many men going up: coming down, about one man per hour from snipers. Brought up fresh supplies of ammunition from Saunders to Battalion Headquarters and reported. Sent troops to lie down: quite exhausted: I sat down and boiled some tea. About 1830 I went up to General Baldwin to report position. C.O. said I must go up on the hill with my other half Company (6, 7) at dusk and hold it for the night. So I made preparations. So tired I could hardly move. About 1800 all of us near Headquarters came in for a lot of shrapnel; a lot of my poor fellows (including Whittome) of 6 and 7 brought in badly wounded. At 1900 I went up with C.O.: he showed me position to take up: too dark to see: I didn't know where enemy was nor who was on flanks. Shone brought half company up about 2000. I put them out and they dug in. Loney dug small pit for Shone and me in centre.

Tuesday, August 10th. I slept most of night. About dawn terrific noise: rifles, machine guns, guns: I didn't know where from or what was doing. We fairly safe in our trenches, but very unsafe to get out. We opened fire on company of Turks trying to rush across cornfield down below. We only had about 10 yards field of fire and view. Suddenly some men of A Company and some men of the — came rushing on to us from in front: we almost shot them. They shouted, " Retire: the Turks are on you." I stopped them and pulled them down into our trenches: as no one from D Company on our right had come, I thought right flank must be safe. So I held on to my position: found out from the fugitives that the — had bolted and a forward trench held by A Company and New Zealanders had had to give way too. This made things rather gloomy for us. However, nothing happened: heavy fire all the time. But about 0545 D Company men came rushing down hill saying the Turks had rushed their trench. I stopped them and wheeled my line to the right so that it faced up hill. Turks didn't come: so we advanced to attack them. We crept up to 40 yards from crest and then started to run. Shone, who was slightly in front, turned back holding his arm, saying " I'm hit." I went on: the men cheered but went up hill slowly. Finally I found no Turks on our side of D Company trenches: so I rushed into them calling on men to man them. Then I found myself in a trench with high sand-bag sides with about six men with me: the rest had stopped and laid down to fire. There were about three bodies in the trench and it was a cul-de-sac: and on looking over parapet I found a group of Turks close up to it. I ducked at once and they fired. Then we bashed at each other across parapet with bayonets, neither side daring to show his head: man next me had whole face blown away. We got picked off one by one ; finally only two men and one shot through shoulder and me left. My bayonet broken by bullet ; took to revolver. I decided to bolt for it : at same time I found by levelling out the corpses we could get back a bit ; also our artillery began dropping H.E. on hill very close to us. So as one burst I leapt out, ran for 10 yards through bullets, threw myself down and rolled down the hill through the scrub to our line. One other man, Pte. Miller, got away. Then I dressed out the line facing up hill again and joined with Hellyer and his men : finally I held the two sides of the spur : Hellyer and his A Company men on left : on right I had about 10 men of three different regiments and put a New Zealand officer in charge. I sent down for reinforcements : nothing came : I had about 30 men left ; both flanks unprotected, so backed about 0900 to head of nullah : grazed on arm by bullet : there three men, including N.Z. officer, immediately sniped from right. Left the New Zealand officer for dead : met him on hospital ship ; stunned by spent bullet. So I withdrew from hill to Headquarters and reported. I never knew who were in rear, who on right and left beyond D and A : nor what the ground was like in front of me. As soon as it got light enough to see the firing made it impossible to reconnoitre.

On way to C.O. found Savage just dead. C.O. asked me if all men were off the hill. I said yes. Then he said, " Tell the men to retire down the main nullah behind next ridge." So we all streamed down : in the nullah at the bad corners people there, as always, said " Run," so the nullah was full of men running to rear for all they were worth. We rallied the Hampshires and Rifles in a cross nullah. Staff Captain Street centre of rallying. Someone asked me why the men were running away. I said they weren't ; and called them all into the cross nullah to prove it (even there men got sniped pretty often) : two officers stood in nullah with revolvers and stopped the rest (not our men) from flying. Very near a panic, but not quite. Then C.O. retired hurt and I took command of the Battalion : only about 100 men and Hellyer left. I started leading them forward again in open order towards the enemy : hills very steep : men exhausted : no one to fire at : great danger of firing on Colonials or Indians or Goorkhas by mistake. We were continually being sniped from every side. Suddenly I felt a blow on thigh and fell down. I told Hellyer to take command. I wondered what the chances were of getting down to the sea alive : about even, I thought. Relieved to find bone not broken. Bandaged it up with a man's help : bullets flicking about all round. Run across a bare patch by two Australians. Then slid and crawled down hill into main (Aghyl) nullah : limped along on two sticks : too many snipers at the corners. Luckily met my servant Wickens, who put on my equipment and helped me down : at bottom of Dere found shrapnel was bursting across the grassland : however, got safe through. Arrived on beach at 1300. Had to stand or lie among crowd of wounded all hustling for places on the boats : no order at all. Two men on stretchers were hit by snipers while lying there. I lay under shelter of a sand bank and slept. Finally got on board the *Neuralia* about 1600. When I had crawled down the companion covered with blood and dust, a steward asked me if I would take afternoon tea.

The difficulties of the fighting were : scarcity of water, combined with very steep hills and hot sun ; the incessant sniping from all sides (you were never absolutely safe at any moment) ; the continuity of it all (fire never ceased day or night). The most disagreeable feature was the general bad smell and the number of rotting bodies.

SOME ACCOUNT OF THE 10th HAMPSHIRE REGIMENT.

By Captain and Quartermaster W. J. Saunders, m.c.

" You have the mark of class about you ! The grand manner in which all of you men have volunteered your services will for ever be a standing credit to your Regiment and to your County traditions, and the whole of the British Empire is proud of you."

These words were spoken by Brig.-General Hill, G.O.C. 31st Infantry Brigade, 10th (Irish) Division, at Beggar's Bush Barracks, Dublin, on 12th September, 1914, to the ten hundred and seventy volunteers from Hampshire, who had responded immediately to Lord Kitchener's call for men, and who had been formed into the 10th Service Battalion The Hampshire Regiment. This Battalion was one of the Units raised in the " First Kitchener Army," and, on formation, was attached to the 10th (Irish) Division as Army Troops. Later, when the 5th (S.) Battalion Royal Irish Regiment was appointed Pioneer Battalion, the 10th Hampshires became part of the 29th Infantry Brigade.

After a short time in Dublin, the Battalion moved to Mullingar, in the County of West Meath, where it was stationed, together with the 11th (S.) Battalion Hampshire Regiment, until March 1915. While stationed at Mullingar many friends were made amongst the local inhabitants. Concerts were organised and parties given to amuse and cheer the troops, and on leaving the town all ranks carried away many very pleasant memories of the people of Mullingar and their kindness towards them. The following is a copy of a letter received from the Town Commissioners :—

" Sir,

I am instructed to forward you the enclosed copy of a Resolution, unanimously adopted at the monthly meeting of the Town Commissioners.

Yours faithfully,

(Signed) P. J. Carroll, *Town Clerk*,

Mullingar."

" Proposed by Mr. P. J. Carey, seconded by Mr. Patrick Brett, and unanimously carried :—

"*Resolved :* That We, The Mullingar Town Commissioners, desire to place on record our fullest appreciation of the very excellent conduct of the troops, comprising the 10th and 11th Hampshire Regiments, since their coming to Mullingar. Considering the large number stationed in the town, a better conducted, more peaceable, and orderly body of soldiers has never before been in this town, and we very heartily congratulate the Commanding Officers of the Battalions on their general good behaviour. When they leave Mullingar they will carry with them the best wishes of the townspeople, and we are confident that when opportunity comes their way, they will be as brave in action as they are gentle in manners."

It may be easily understood that the behaviour of the men while at Mullingar must have been considerably influenced by the hearty welcome on arrival, and the great kindness extended to them during their stay, and therefore a part of the Town Commissioners' appreciation was most deservedly due to those of the inhabitants who were instrumental in making things go so well. Chief amongst those who made themselves responsible for, and assisted in the entertainment of the troops, the following ladies will be remembered :—

> The Misses Tottenham, of Tudenham Park.
> Mrs. Robertson.
> „ Patrick.
> „ Hyde.
> Miss Hyde.
> „ Dowdall.
> „ Chauney.
> „ Kelly, of Athlone, and
> „ Betty O'Doherty.

The last mentioned vocalist was a great favourite of the men. The haunting refrains of her songs, " Connemara," " Mother Machree " and " The Bugler Boy," all of which she rendered in character so charmingly, made a great impression upon all ranks of the Battalion, and were remembered by many of them, even unto " the end."

The Battalion left Mullingar in March 1915 and joined the 29th Infantry Brigade at the Rath Camp, Curragh. The other battalions of the Brigade were the 6th (S.) Battalion Royal Irish Rifles, 5th (S.) Battalion Connaught Rangers, and the 6th (S.) Battalion Leinster Regiment. The Brigade was Commanded by Brig.-General R. J. Cooper, c.v.o. Issue of Service rifles, Vickers guns and the new-pattern leather equipment was made here. A few days of Brigade Training were undergone. General Sir Bryan Mahon, G.O.C. 10th (Irish) Division, held an inspection, and then at the end of May the Battalion moved to Basingstoke Common, where the whole Division concentrated. The other two Infantry Brigades of the 10th (Irish) Division were the 30th and 31st. These were composed of the first Service Battalions of Irish Regiments, so that the 10th (S.) Battalion Hampshire Regiment was the only other than Irish Battalion in the Division. The month of June was occupied in Divisional exercises, billeting schemes, and manœuvres, particularly night work. While at Basingstoke the men of the Battalion were very pleased to receive a gift of a small parcel of smokes, sent to each of them with the " Best Wishes of the Ladies of Ireland."

On July 7th the Battalion embarked on H.M.T. *Transylvania* at Liverpool, the other units on board being Headquarters 29th Infantry Brigade, 5th (S.) Battalion Royal Irish Regiment (less one Company), 6th (S.) Battalion Royal Irish Rifles, 109th Company A.S.C., and 30th Field Ambulance. Gibraltar was reached on the 11th, Malta on the 14th, and Alexandria on the 17th. Leaving Alexandria on the evening of the 19th, Lemnos was reached on the 21st, and the Battalion disembarked at Turk's Head Point on the following day. The journey, so far, needs no further description. Except for the precautions of following a zig-zag course, and " darkened " ship, the voyage was the same as that of a transport in peace time. Lemnos was beyond description. There was at that time no accommodation for the troops whatever. The sun was very powerful, and fresh water hard to obtain. Flies were there in their billions, latrines were open and inoculation rife. But still the troops cheered when they heard that the road to Baghdad " was now open ! " A communiqué from the Tigris had brought news of some success to our arms, which, it said, " laid open the road to Baghdad," and the end was in sight. The thrilling sound of that Minden yell must have been heard at Ctesiphon.

After a few days, per M.H.T. *Abbasieh*, the Battalion moved on to Anzac, where the 29th Infantry Brigade was attached to the Australian and New Zealand Army Corps. While on the Peninsula the Battalion took part in the actions Sari Bair, August 8th to 14th, and Hill 60, or Kabak Kuyu, August 21st : holding in the interval the position known as Goorkha Trenches. Withdrawal from Anzac took place on 29th September, embarkation, under cover of darkness, being effected at Walker's Pier. During the eight weeks that the Battalion served at Anzac the casualties approximated 30 officers and 800 other ranks. With the remainder of 29th Infantry Brigade the Battalion now returned to Mudros to find that the 30th and 31st Infantry Brigades, together with 10th Divisional Headquarters, had withdrawn from Suvla Bay and concentrated there also. Welcome reinforcements, both officers and men, met the Battalion at Mudros.

Landing at Salonica during the first week in October 1915, the Battalion next found itself to be a part of the first British formation to set foot in Macedonia. The Regimental Transport, which had remained at Basingstoke on the Battalion's departure, now rejoined. After a few parades, and a couple of grabs at the ordnance and remount dumps, the Battalion entrained for Doiran, and in the first week of December found itself upon the east end of the Kosturino Ridge in the south-east of Serbia, endeavouring to hold up, or delay, the Austro-Bulgar advance. In the action at Kajali the Battalion suffered about

300 casualties : this number inclusive of about 70 taken prisoner, the survivors of which met the Battalion at Strumitza on its victorious march into Bulgaria in 1918. Withdrawing, *via* Dedeli Pass and Doiran, the Battalion arrived at Salonica on 22nd December, encamping alongside the Monastir Road. A brief respite from movement permitted the Season of Peace and Goodwill to be observed and the most was made of local resources. The time-honoured hardy annual soccer match, Officers and Sergeants, was even remembered.

After a brief halt, spent mainly in refitting, the Battalion embarked upon H.M.T. *Partridge* on 29th December and proceeded to Stavros on the south-west shore of the Rendina Gulf. The writer of *Salonica and After* describes this place as " One of the most favoured spots in Macedonia." We agree. At the time of our arrival, Stavros could offer the much buffeted troops of the 29th Infantry Brigade neither billet, tent, nor bivouac, but it welcomed our landing with a burst of brilliant sunshine, the cheering warmth of which speedily dispelled from our midst the gloom of having again failed, and Serbia 1915 became apparently forgotten. The position we had now taken up proved to be the right flank of the Salonica Birdcage Line, and much labour was undertaken in strengthening it against the then greatly talked of " push them into the sea " German-Bulgar offensive, which was to clear the whole of the Allies out of the Balkans.

In February 1916 the 29th was relieved by the 80th Infantry Brigade of the 27th Division, and we moved by march route *via* the south side of Beshik and Langaza Lakes to Aivasil. Here the Battalion was employed in improving communications and about a month was spent working on the so-called roads on the Aivasil and Azrameri Hills. Divisional concentration on Hortiach plateau, above the village of Kapudzilar was the next move and Brigade and Divisional training was indulged in with much zest. The Battalion was now issued with its first two Lewis guns, the two Vickers being handed over to the Brigade M.G. Company. It will be interesting to note that at the time of disbandment the number of Lewis guns had been increased to 32 per Battalion. Some football matches and boxing contests were held, in both of which the Battalion did well. About the end of May the Battalion, with remainder of 29th Brigade, moved by march route from Hortiach to Orljak Bridge on the Struma River. Following a spell of rather cool weather, a great heat set in on the first day of the march, which proved very exhausting to the troops. Several fatal casualties occurred in the Brigade, the Battalion losing Pte. Tunks, who succumbed at the end of the first day's march. The following extract is from *Salonica and After* :—

" On one of the last days of May 1916 I happened to be a short distance up-country along the Langaza Valley. One of the Battalions which had been holding the line of hills there, some eight or ten miles out of Salonica, had organised an assault-at-arms, and I was invited to see the fun. There was a marquee with refreshments, and everything went off splendidly. But in the middle of the Sports the 10th (Irish) Division began to file past, on their way to take up the line on the far Struma. It was a blistering hot day and the men with their heavy packs had marched down from the high plateau just under Mt. Hortiach. They marched slowly past in a cloud of dust, every man looking at the trim enclosure of the Sports ground, with its marquee and chairs and general look of happiness. The Tenth had come from Gallipoli and already had experience of what a Balkan winter could be. And as they walked past now, beads of sweat hanging big on the face of every man and the dust swirling about their feet, they gave us the first real hint of what campaigning in a Balkan summer was likely to be."

On reaching the valley the Battalion took up the line along the Struma River from Orljak Bridge eastward to what we afterwards recognised as Jungle Island. The work here consisted chiefly of preparing a defensive line, at which the Battalion continued until the end of July. Neither Bulgar nor Turk worried us during this period, but an enemy against which we had but little defence was very active. The hum of the myriads of mosquito sounded at night like the drone of distant aeroplane engines and lucky indeed was the individual who escaped the consequences of their attentions. The Battalion was very careful in the regular taking of quinine and whilst actually on the river line did not suffer nearly so heavily as some other units, but nevertheless a considerable number of casualties took place through malaria. After about eight weeks in the valley the Battalion was relieved by the Royal Inniskilling Fusiliers and marched down the Seres Road towards Salonica, taking up position in the Birdcage Line above Ajvatli on the immediate west of the Derbend which connects Lembet with the Langaza valley. Malaria now came out rather badly and many casualties took place. The head-dress was here exchanged, the slouch hat being replaced by helmet. The next move was to Dremiglava, more generally recognised perhaps as " The Vineyard." Here the troops were bivouacked in a large field plentifully stocked with vines and other fruit trees. As the gathering of fruit was strictly forbidden, the luscious peaches, figs and grapes were left upon the trees until they ripened and fell off : into open hands ! A change of first line transport was now made, all wheel being replaced by pack. The loading of the pack animals had not then been advanced to the almost fine art which it afterwards became, and during the practices and inspections which took place it was not an uncommon occurrence for an alarmed mule to break loose and proceed to make a distribution of its load along the Brigade front, the load generally proving to be one or another of the Company Officer's Messes.

In September another move forward to the Struma was made. Owing to the weakness of the units caused by malaria casualties, it was found necessary to reduce each Battalion to one Company, and the Infantry Brigade thus consisted of a Composite Battalion made up of one Company from each of its Infantry units. We found the personnel for Battalion Headquarters and also the first line transport, the Composite Battalion being Commanded by Lieut.-Colonel J. D. M. Beckett, D.S.O. The details which were not required for running this Composite Battalion were sent back to the camp at Dremiglava, and as reinforcements became available the Battalions were reorganised to two, three, and eventually back to four Companies again. This, however, was not completed until the beginning of the year 1917. On reaching the Struma we found ourselves relieving the French in the Dimitric Sector, and holding the River Line from Komarjan Bridge to Gudeli Ford. The presence of the enemy near the north bank of the river had now become a threat upon the bridge-head position, and he had therefore to be dislodged. The Battalion took part in the engagements at Komarjan, Dzamimah, Karadzakoi Zir and Karadzakoi Bala, and Yenikoi. The enemy made spirited attempts to retake these villages, but failed. Our casualties were light, but we lost Lieut. Tanner killed and Lieut. Wilson severely wounded.

In November 1916 the Battalion left its comrades of the 10th (Irish) Division and was transferred to the 27th Division, joining the 82nd Infantry Brigade which consisted of the 2nd Battalion D.C.L.I., 2nd Battalion Gloucestershire Regiment, and 10th Cameron Highlanders (Lovat's Scouts), and took part in the operations against the enemy position at Tumbitza Farm on the north bank of the Meander River. As a front line, the Struma River bank was now abandoned, and the 82nd Infantry Brigade advanced and took up the line Yenimah - Osman Kamilla, the right flank practically resting upon the marshes at the north-west end of the Tahinos Lake. This advance permitted the use of the several unoccupied villages in the area, and enabled the Battalion to be placed in billets for the first time since June 1915. In the following June this front line was demolished and a line of redoubts built to cover the various bridge-heads which had now been made along the river. The right, or south, bank of the river was held thinly, and the bulk of the troops withdrawn to the high ground south of the valley to escape the mosquito as much as possible. During the following November the Battalion, with the remainder of the 82nd Infantry Brigade, moved by march route to the Neohori Sector at the east end of the Tahinos Lake, where the River Struma empties into the Gulf of Orfano. This position was about 16 miles along the coast, north of Stavros, where the Battalion landed in December 1915. The advance to this position was made in 1916 when the Struma Line was taken up. This right flank of the Allied Front was now held jointly with the Royal Navy. Several cruisers, monitors, and other smaller boats, lay in the bay, and an aerodrome of the R.N.A.S. was established near Vrasta at a point which afterwards became known as Eastchurch. The Battalion, on arrival, took over the Bluff Camp position, and subsequently the K.C. sub-sector immediately above Hall's Bridge. This bridge, built by the Royal Engineers, spanned the Struma just where it opened out before entering the marshes at Cajezi, and was situate immediately south of the buried ruins of Amphipolis.

While holding this position the Battalion lost, on 9th February, 1917, through a sad accident, its Commanding Officer, Lieut.-Colonel J. D. M. Beckett, D.S.O. This officer had held Command of the Battalion since taking over in Serbia in November 1915, and he was very well known throughout the British line. His cheerfulness, even under the most trying circumstances, was an outstanding characteristic of his life, while his kindly consideration for all with whom he came in contact made him the idol of his own men, and endeared him to all others. The following is a copy of a letter received from a former Brigade Commander :—

"65 Dorset Road,
Bexhill-on-Sea.
February 23rd, 1918.

" Dear Taylor,
I have just read, with the very deepest of regret, the announcement of Lieut.-Colonel Beckett's death, and I cannot refrain from sending a line to his Regiment to express my great sorrow.

During my year's Command of the 82nd Brigade I had full opportunity of appreciating his very high military qualifications, but apart from this, I always found him a true and staunch friend, and I know that his popularity in the Battalion he commanded so well was unbounded. His loss will be felt throughout the Brigade, but more especially, of course, in the Battalion. As an old friend of most of your officers, will you express to them my regret for the loss they have sustained.

We can ill spare soldiers of Colonel Beckett's stamp.

Yours sincerely,
C. M. MAYNARD.

" The O.C.,
10th Hampshire Regiment."

This gallant officer was buried on the north bank of the Struma River immediately behind the position held by the Battalion, and a little below Hall's Bridge. Representatives of all neighbouring units attended, and aeroplanes from the R.N.A.S. Squadron at Stavros circled above whilst the burial was taking place. As one brother for another, so mourned every officer and soldier of the Battalion his sad loss.

During the following June our Greek allies took over the front held by our (27th) Division. The 82nd Brigade was withdrawn, and moved *via* Stavros - Guvesne - Karasouli, rejoining our Division at Dreveno on the right bank of the Vardar River. This move was made on the Decauville line from Stavros, through the Rendina gorge and Langaza valley to Sarakli, thence by the broad gauge to Salamanli, where the military extension joined the Salonika - Vardar Valley Line, and then up the valley to within about three miles of the town of Guevgheli, then held by the Bulgar. This movement, it will be noted, cleared us completely from the Struma Valley, which we had occupied for over two years, and took our Division from the right to the left flank of the British line. Although this change extended the front across the Vardar to the westward, the line actually held was reduced from a 100 to about 70 miles. From west to east our Divisions were now placed 27th, 26th, 22nd and 28th. The front which the 27th Division now took up had previously been held by our French allies. On arrival at the new front the Battalion was placed in Divisional Reserve in the Cascades and Pactol ravines, behind the villages of Kara Sinanci and Mayadag. During the latter part of August a careful course of preparation was undertaken in readiness for an attack upon the enemy salient La Roche Noire, near the village of Alcar Mahale. In extent this salient was about a thousand yards in frontage, and of the same depth, and from front to rear consisted of rocky heights and sharply-defined ravines. It was very strongly entrenched and simply bristled with trench mortars and machine guns. It had been attacked and taken by the French about a year previous, but as it was commanded by the enemy battery positions from behind and on both flanks, the concentrated gun-fire made it too expensive to hold. Model plans of this position were made upon the Vardar sands. Every item of information which could be gleaned by ground scout or aerial observation was displayed in plan. The position of wires, trenches, trench-mortar and machine-gun emplacements, and pill-boxes, were outlined for the information of all concerned. Every officer and soldier engaged was told confidentially what was being planned, and what his particular job was to be, the only item of information which was withheld until later being the date and time of the assault.

This took place at 1730 hours on September 1st, and proved to be the opening of the offensive which brought success to the Allies in Macedonia. Two Battalions were engaged in this little operation. The 2nd Battalion Gloucester Regiment assaulted and captured the Montaux Buissons on the right of the salient, whilst we on the left did the same with the positions La Table, La Roche Noire, Les Deux Roches, Dos de Mulet, and the Tranchée des Roches. An element of surprise was prepared for the Bulgar in that our advance took place without the somewhat usual covering barrage, and our leading waves were closing upon his front posts before he got his guns going. The enemy made desperate attempts to retake the salient early the following morning after an intense bombardment throughout the night, but thanks to the knowledge gained during the preparation in August, we were ready to deny him, and although he did regain a footing on our side of the salient, we countered him out, and he did not come up again. In this operation the Battalion lost in killed and wounded four officers, Capt. W. A. Lowy, Lieut. W. B. Sparrow, Lieut. A. E. Fishlock, killed, and Lieut. W. H. Collins, wounded, and about 200 other ranks. The casualties approximated about 60 per cent. of the Battalion's fighting strength. The Commanding Officer, Lieut.-Col. T. E. H. Taylor, M.C., Royal Irish Regiment, was rewarded with the D.S.O. and Captains Grellier and Green and Lieut. W. H. Collins with the Military Cross. Six other ranks received the Military Medal, and the Battalion was complimented by the General Officer Commanding in Chief upon its gallantry in this small but nevertheless important action. The attack was now taken up on the left by the French and Serbian forces and on the right by our remaining Divisions and the Greek forces, resulting in the Bulgars' defeat and rapid retreat. The Battalion, with 27th Division, advanced to Dubnitza, about two days' march from Sofia, when orders were received for the Division to return to Base and prepare for movement to S. Russia.

On the departure of the 27th Division from Salonica the Battalion was changed into the 22nd Division for a short while, and afterwards joined the 28th Division at Constantinople. The signing of the Armistice led to the hasty demobilisation of the Forces and the Battalion, after absorbing the 8th D.C.L.I. and 10th Devons, was disbanded early in 1920.

War diary account of operations undertaken by 10th Bn. The Hampshire Regiment on 1st and 2nd September, 1918.
    Ref. 1/20,000 Mayadag sheet.
    1/5000 Div. Operation Map No. 1, Ed. II.

On **1st September, 1918,** the 10th Hampshire Regt., together with 2nd Gloucester Regt., assaulted and captured the Roche Noire salient. The following is an account of the battle. Punctually at 1730 hours Companies " jumped off " to attack. The Companies were allotted objectives as follows :—

    A Company—
        (i) Enemy front line at junction of Boyau de Danube with Eleonore Trench, to seize the whole of the Boyau de Danube C.T., taking the eastern half of New Eleonore Trench *en route*.
        (ii) Two platoons to attack Les Deux Roches position.
        (iii) One platoon to attack Le Dos de Mulet position.

C Company—

(i) To penetrate enemy front line on left of A Company and to capture the western half of New Eleonore Trench.

(ii) To capture La Roche Noire *point d'appui*, seizing work C 99 *en route*.

(iii) One platoon to assault and capture the Tranchée des Roches.

D Company : To capture the remainder of La Table and the work known as Les Taupes. B Company was in Battalion Reserve. At 1758 hours Battalion Headquarters advanced to pt. C 113 a. The situation was then as follows :—A Company on the point of capturing Les Deux Roches ; C Company about to capture La Roche Noire ; D Company in possession of La Table except for Pt. C 112 b, where Bulgar bombers were still holding out. D Company pressed home their attack and quickly captured this post without loss. At 1810 hours A and C Companies had captured the main objectives of Les Deux Roches and La Roche Noire respectively, A Company taking 28 prisoners and C Company taking 12 prisoners and one machine gun. By 2100 hours Dos de Mulet and Tr. des Roches positions were in our hands, thus completing the capture of the whole of the Battalion's objectives.

During the assault the enemy maintained an intense barrage on his front. B Company, in reserve, suffered severe casualties during this period. Communication was only possible by runner, a slow and difficult method owing to the broken nature of the ground and the heavy fire to which the runners were subjected. As soon as it was dusk, consolidation was begun and was pushed on in spite of continuous heavy gun shell-fire, the work of carrying parties especially being hindered. Working parties took some time to organise owing to casualties sustained.

At this juncture strengths of Companies were reported to be as follows :—

A Company	...	59	all ranks, with	6	L.G.'s.
B ,,	...	58	,, ,,	3	,,
C ,,	...	51	,, ,,	3	,,
D ,,	...	42	,, ,,	3	,,

A Company reinforced by two platoons of B Company, formed the garrison of the whole of the captured position. The remainder of B Company, under Capt. Lowy, was sent to reconnoitre Tr. du Saillant. C Company assembled at La Roche Noire preparatory to withdrawal to Parallel 2. D Company moved to Raviné and relieved a Company of the 4th Bn. Rifle Brigade in the front line. At 0428 hours the enemy put down a sudden and intense barrage. C Company was at once ordered to man La Roche Noire. At 0445 hours Capt.

Lowy's patrol returned and reported enemy movement up Ravin des Deux Roches.

At 0455 hours a hostile counter-attack developed against Les Deux Roches from the N. and N.E., accompanied by an exceedingly heavy bombardment of Les Deux Roches, La Table and Les Taupes. At 0500 hours enemy pressed home his attack against Les Deux Roches. Two platoons, under Capt. Green, immediately delivered a successful counter-attack on Les Deux Roches, from which the enemy was driven just as he was gaining a footing on the northern slope. The position was cleared by 0530 hours, leaving the whole of the objectives allotted to the Battalion securely in our hands.

T. E. H. TAYLOR, *Lieut.-Col.*
Cmdg. 10th Bn. Hampshire Regt.

17/9/18.

EXTRACTS FROM A LETTER

Written by G.O.C. 27th Division, in which were 10th Bn. Hampshire Regiment, to G.O.C. 26th Division, in which were 12th Bn. Hampshire Regiment, and published for information of 12th Bn. Hampshire Regiment.

" I witnessed the attack from a position overlooking, and comparatively close to, the position assaulted, and until the fog of dust and smoke became impenetrable I watched the Battalion. I have never seen a battalion advance more steadily or behave more gallantly than did the 10th Hampshires. Six separate objectives had to be taken, and the various advances and changes of direction were performed as if on parade, and under a very heavy artillery fire.

The dash of the men was extraordinary, as was also their resolution and tenacity during the heavy shelling which they received during consolidation, and in the overthrow of the enemy's counter-attack.

I am proud to command such a Battalion, and every man belonging to the Hampshire Regiment can feel a legitimate pride in the gallantry displayed by one of its Battalions."

(See also Appendix I of Major W. S. Cowland's Narrative, page 75.)

WITH THE 10TH AND 12TH BATTALIONS THE HAMPSHIRE REGIMENT, MACEDONIA, 1916–18.

By MAJOR W. S. COWLAND, D.S.O.

1916.

18 Feb. H.M.T. *Olympic*. Started late last night. Wireless messages to the effect that there is nothing doing, nor likely to be doing, at Salonika. But why all these troops ? Australians on board buying from the stewards turkeys for 15*s*. each, and two chickens for 10*s*.

23 Feb. Mild excitement this morning : two alarms in quick succession, but apparently dodged the submarine. Hear later that a torpedo was fired, but was about 1,000 yards away.

1 Mar. Alexandria. Disembarked yesterday morning and reported at Base. Hicks and I are staying at Villa Yasmin awaiting next move by sea.

27 Mar. Work of the mildest, though we have been able to give assistance to distressed officers wanting their kits, which had in many cases parted company with them at the time of the evacuation of Gallipoli, and hear to-day we may move to Salonika about the middle of the week. Have now moved to Bulkeley Parsonage. Work in the kit-shed varied with sea-bathing from the house, and expeditions.

1 Apr. Hortiach Plateau. 10th Battalion The Hampshire Regt. Arrived at Salonika yesterday morning, and disembarked soon after mid-day. Then a long march right through the town eastwards to where the 10th Division are, some 10 miles, and nearly all uphill through country rather like the West Highlands, till about 7 p.m., when arrived at our destination on the shoulder of a mountain. A very pleasant spot, more than 1,000 feet above sea level, with a view over the harbour. In Corps Reserve, and mainly occupied with fatigues and brigade training. Hicks has B Company and I have A Company. Lieut.-Col. J. D. M. Beckett, D.S.O., 1st Battalion The Hampshire Regiment, is commanding, and Major Davies of the Royal Warwickshire Regiment is second in command. Chase looks after our Company Mess very efficiently. Of the original 10th Battalion, Clement, Scott, Saunders, Dupree are here.

9 Apr. Still in the same camp. Excitements are few, though a German aeroplane had a look round the other day, and afterwards returned northwards. Inspections are the order of the day, everything from boots to a round of ammunition. A very good pamphlet,

Notes on Balkan Warfare, by Brig.-Gen. P. Howell of the General Staff, and author of the admirable book on the Campaign in Thrace, 1912, has just been issued. A Company's four platoon commanders are Chase, Harfield, Carruthers, and Green, who is also bombing officer.

10 Apr. Ajvasil. Orders just in from Brigade that a Company of Hampshires were to go out to Ajvasil for five days for digging second line defences. A Company was selected, and here we are, with cooks and transport all complete. Lines overlook a big lake, Lake Langaza, and to the mountains beyond. Rations will come out each day and a small canteen will be possible ; also lake bathing. Behind there is a gully for water supply. Except for work under the R.E., we are on our own. There are a few gunners and a veterinary place near by, otherwise miles from anyone.

12 Apr. Still enjoying life at the same place, digging all day and football or a sing-song in the evening. Rode down to the village on the lake yesterday afternoon to get some Greek notes changed for the canteen ; nothing much in it, but a nice tree with storks building in the branches. First the frogs and then jackals give entertainment at night.

14 Apr. Hortiach Plateau. Back from work at Ajvasil last night. Had to mount an enormous hill made by the British. No one in the Company fell out, which is promising for trek next week. Gale has just sprung up. No flies yet. Next week is going to be glorified manœuvres, marching, hill piqueting, perimeter camps, and such like. At present spending the time over a thousand and one details, from mules to slouch hats. All been issued with hats like the Australians and Boy Scouts wear. Have seen some orders issued to 39th (Reserve) Corps, German. Their instructions were entirely how to meet French and Russian attacks ; the British were not even mentioned.

25 Apr. First anniversary of Gallipoli Landing. Brigade manœuvres did not start till Wednesday, though all arrangements were made by Sunday night. Monday broke a pouring wet day, and after standing by for hours, orders from Brigade that operations were deferred till Wednesday. Practically all transport is done by pack mules, and everyone is anxiously thinking out number of ropes for loading blankets, ammunition, picks and shovels, and water-carriers. Arrived at starting point, about three miles eastwards of camp, with guns, R.E., A.S.C., R.A.M.C., and all other units attached to the Brigade. B and C Companies told off to piquet the heights, the Hampshire Regiment being advanced guard. A Company were with Battalion H.Q., so except for supporting a few of the piquets going up the hills came off rather lightly the first day, and had little to do but foot-slog it along the road. Roads are sometimes little more than tracks where one has to go single file for perhaps eight miles, but sometimes real roads which have been made in the side of mountains by the British. What constantly amazes is the enormous amount of work that has been done.

Wednesday night bivouacked near Adrameri, a pretty little village perched on a hill. Thursday the Hampshires in the main body, and moved on through perfect country to Zagliveri ; Irish Regiments to-day piqueting the heights, and doing advanced guard. Arrived in about 2.30 p.m. rather tired ; had orders to go out to a line of hills to the north and put out night outposts. Moved off in a quarter of an hour, as had to get the Company up to the hills, see the ground, and have piquets out before dusk. C.O. thought three piquets would be required, so three platoons went out under Chase, Harfield and Sergt. Payne to the obvious hills, and went on myself to look over the ground before dark. Carruthers stayed behind to bring along the pack mules, with blankets, ammunition, tools and water. Then the trouble began. His orders were to press up the gully until he came to Company H.Q., which were likely to be somewhere near the top of gully behind middle piquet. Some man told him H.Q. would be a long way down the gully ; result, at 7 p.m. no mules had turned up, only Carruthers, looking very hot and dishevelled. He reported mules had had to return to camp by 7 p.m. and all our stuff was dumped three-quarters of a mile down the gully. All the piquets were by this time out and digging in with entrenching tools and sangaring, so H.Q. had to carry blankets, etc., up gully, where they were distributed among the three piquets. Men worked finely, staggering with ammunition boxes over the most appalling ravines, and by 11.30 p.m. piquets were supplied with immediate necessities, and were visited and found to be all correct. Returned to H.Q. about 1 a.m. and found the boy who had been looking after my horse had allowed it to walk off into the darkness, so could only hope it had walked back to camp. About 4 a.m. a message through by lamp that it had returned safely to camp. Morning broke, and orders came from Brigade to " report immediately to Brigade H.Q. at head of column "—then from C.O., " Report immediately at Hampshires H.Q." Selected the latter first, Chase meanwhile closing up the piquets on the right and following. On arrival at H.Q. was told A Company was in support of C Company in an attack on " Bare Hill," which was on no map. Company arrived breakfastless through no one's fault, and after many adventures amongst gullies arrived in time for final assault.

Hicks and I hope to ride in and lunch with Mr. Pallis at Salonika next Sunday. Shall take the opportunity of seeing something of the place. Pallis signs himself " Secretary General Refugees Commission " : do not gather as yet that he is British Consul, but he may be. Very hot weather but not yet the flies : there ought to be more chance of coping with them here than on the Peninsula. Life in Greece is good so far. Camp arrangements are all excellent. Very difficult country, gullies and mountains, and an advance seems doubtful; but if the enemy attacks he should get a hot reception. A good many E. Surrey and 3rd Sussex men out in drafts. Very good 3rd Sussex boy is now acting as my orderly and servant, Peacock by name. Thorough with his work, and knows all about horses. The General gave a long talk last night on the manœuvres: seemed pleased on the whole, though had some severish criticisms on ammunition supply, which depends on the pack mules and their management.

27 Apr. Yesterday morning the storm began, raged all day and got worse in the night.

On Tuesday evening Hicks and I went to Kirekeui, about two miles off, and practised modern Greek, or rather Hicks did most of the talking. Easter celebrations were being kept up, with dancing on village green under the plane tree, which is found in most villages: very slow and simple dance, accompanied by a gentleman playing on a kind of bagpipe made from a goat skin; only five notes to the tune.

3 May. Hicks and I rode into Salonika on Sunday; bought a very fine and comfortable pair of local shoes, lunched with Mr. Pallis, who is Overseer of Refugees from round Smyrna and from Macedonia. He gave us a very good lunch at his Club and afterwards took us round the four best churches, St. Sophia, St. George, Holy Friday and St. Demetrius; in the last-named they hold the State Service, attended by the King, once a year, on the day Salonika was taken from the Turks, 1912. The Turks did a good deal of damage when they turned the churches into mosques, with the result that few of the frescoes are in anything like good condition. It looks odd to see a church with a minaret by its side. At St. George's a christening was going on, and received a 5 lepta piece from father of infant, as having been witnesses of the ceremony. Ride home across the mountains in cool of evening.

5 May. More firing on the range to-day; on arrival back heard news of Zeppelin brought down on the Vardar Marshes by a 9.2 inch gun from a monitor, direct hit.

15 May. Last Sunday Hicks, Ivor Powell and I went up big mountain near by, Hortiach Dag, a stiffish and hot climb, but view well worth trouble. A wonderfully beautiful country that we looked down upon. Unfortunately could just not see the three prongs of Chalcidice—nor Mount Athos.

On Monday, A and B Companies went off for a week's quarrying and road-making. Four hours in morning, three in afternoon. Quarry was a better spot than road, as work on latter place carried on under difficulties with transport passing up and down hill continuously.

23 May. Salonika most interesting; saw the remains of the Zeppelin, now nothing but scrap-iron; officers and soldiers of all sorts; town full of Serbs; was much impressed by them and their fine looks. Rumours are rife, one moment for France, next for Mesopotamia, next for Alexandretta.

29 May. Down by the Lake again, probably going up the hill to-morrow. Faith, original Adjutant of the 10th, has arrived back again; is commanding D Company at present. Working hours are now 5.30 - 6.30 and 7.30 - 10.30 a.m., and 3 - 6 p.m.; it is warming up, but there is still much green about and the place is a mass of wild flowers. However hot it gets it will be very different from Lemnos or the sun-baked Peninsula. The C.O. is away for two days looking at the Serbian Army.

9 June. The Battalion in camp 5 miles south of Orljak Bridge. Last Sunday (June 4) we moved off from our comfortable quarters and took three days moving up country, along the Seres Road, still with the object of road-making. Two days of the march were very hot and the men suffered considerably. The poor infantryman carries a most terrible amount on him, and in this stewing weather, with the men still on the winter scale equipment, it is not surprising that a certain number were completely knocked out. Tuesday arrived at our destination and went into a standing camp; told to settle down for three weeks. Something may be going to happen here: anyhow one does feel we are ready: things look properly managed.

News of Naval Battle (Jutland) and death of Kitchener have come in the telegrams—but more news is awaited. The *Balkan News* gives a good idea of what is happening. The flies are becoming a great nuisance, though nothing else to complain of. Good to see the Russians moving again in Galicia; that fact, following on Austrian attack in Trentino, looks as if the Allies have at last a definite policy. The enemy's persistence at Verdun, the Naval Battle, and Austrian attack all encouraging.

11 June. By a piece of luck ran into our Second in Command last night, who went into hospital ten days ago, but I did not know what hospital. He also is getting out to-morrow, and has made all arrangements for us both. Get taken by field ambulance into Salonika early to-morrow morning, and on Tuesday morning up to the front in a motor lorry, about 40 miles to go, in order to get to where I believe the Regiment is. All in Salonika is pretty normal and quiet, in spite of wild reports. The Greeks will apparently remain neutral and are demobilizing. Sarrail is Commanding-in-Chief, and General Milne G.O.C. the British. I love this country more and more. Everything is looking lovely this quiet Sunday afternoon, though guns boom out Doiran way fairly continuously. A French aerodrome near us here, and machines constantly going up.

13 June. Yesterday the Field Ambulance took us into Salonika early; fixed up with A.S.C. Base Supply Depot to get a lift out to 72nd kilo. on Seres Road, and left heavy kit with them. On to Hotel Olympus and booked room for night; spent a fairly quiet day doing odd shopping, lunched and dined at White Tower. Had a very agreeable evening sitting in White Tower Gardens overlooking the Harbour and listening to a Greek band. Spent the afternoon sleeping in smoking room of Hotel Olympus; in moments of wakefulness listened to an old Serb officer sitting at the piano trying to pick out Funeral March movement of the Chopin Sonata. Serb army is a very live thing. The officers particularly look a smart and capable lot—they ought to be the latter, for (as one remarked) they have been fighting off and on for years and it had become their normal form of existence. Salonika rather attractive, though a dirty town. Pleasant sitting at a café, and watching the life which is full of interest. Just back with the Battalion after a 72-kilo. ride on a very lumpy road on a smelly A.S.C. motor lorry. Bulgars are on hills opposite, a long way across Struma Valley. We are still peace training (hours 3.30 - 5 or 6 a.m., and 7 - 8.30 p.m.) and no excitements.

14 June. On Struma between Orljak Bridge and Sakavca. Very hot, but have comfortable booth made of branches, covered with waterproof sheet and blankets, which keep off a lot of sun. Mosquitoes pretty bad in this place, which is comparatively low-lying compared with former residences. If net tucked round the head at night comes off, sure enough next morning there is a lump on forehead or eyelid; fortunately do not seem very virulent and bumps soon go down. By day a flyswish during waking hours and a net whilst dozing keep the flies fairly tame. Yesterday Hicks and I rode down to the river (1) to bathe, (2) to reconnoitre the country. Turks and Bulgars and all manner of Macedonian mongrels seem very peaceful, looking after their crops and cattle, but one never can be quite certain who is a komitadji in disguise. A very nice bathe in the stream which figures in Thucydides' works in connection with Amphipolis. A fordable stream in many places, a pretty good dividing line, with the Salonika - Constantinople Railway beyond. If we stop as far forward next winter the Seres Road, our sole line of communication, will be severely tested during a wet season, though pretty passable now for lorries with the large amount of care bestowed upon it and them. All is quiet here: except for inspections and drill, physical training half-hour, the men are let down fairly easily; they get plenty of time for bathing and keeping themselves and their belongings clean. Our main difficulty will be to keep everyone fit during the summer, or the story of Gallipoli sickness will be repeated. How many sick left the Peninsula per day last August and September?

18 June. Waterloo Day. Yesterday mounted officers of the Regiment did a staff ride out to the front along a line which will probably be taken over soon : started at 5 a.m., arrived back at 4 p.m.—a long day in the saddle, but interesting and instructive. At one village Hicks and I discovered some boys who did not know there was a great European War on : an old lady, whom I judged to be a Bulgar or Turk, gave me a very nice drink of water. Some of the peasants have never heard of the Great Powers, or Great Britain : all they want is to be left in peace to till their land. One of the small boys on being further questioned thought we might be Turkish soldiers, but he really did not know. On enquiring when there was likely to be rain again, he answered, " God above alone knows." This day (18 June) last year I remember writing a letter from a hole in the cliff near W Beach at Cape Helles.

21 June. The Battalion moved to Orljak Bridge and formed a defensive line making a bridge-head.

24 June. Weather extremely hot, culminating in severe thunderstorm accompanied by a heavy downpour, which was appreciated. A and B Companies have moved camp once more and are back at Headquarters. The last four days have been full of spies, bridgeheads, night outposts, patrols, frogs, mosquitoes, storks, and spies in motors. It ended this morning, and C and D Companies took over. Had a very good vegetable dish the other day in a Greek house ; it consisted of marrow, flour, oil and garlic. Storks sit on the tops of trees about here ; " Josey " nearly shot me off the other day when one flapped past within a few yards of her nose. Have spent last few nights with frogs hopping over me and tortoises crawling around. The latter one can count by thousands, little black heads sticking out of the water.

27 June. Near Komarian, on river bank. Carrying out wiring operations for the defence of a bridge-head. Digging operations in progress at the same time, for which I am only partly responsible. Have a battalion to work with each day, and once parties are told off and tools drawn work goes fairly smoothly. Chief trouble is that different battalions come each day, with the result that time is wasted going over the same ground with a different lot of officers, the wiring being of rather an unusual pattern. Then the limbers which bring stakes from a wood three-quarters of a mile off sometimes fail us, so that the old horse works pretty hard most of the morning moving from place to place. Hope we shall not be moved before we have been able to shew we have made a good job of it. Other parties are in the trenches and patrolling at night. Greece is still an excellent place, *i.e.* Eastern Macedonia : plenty of green, not like the horrible and sandy Gallipoli Peninsula. The interpreter gets us eggs from a Greek village, contrary to the orders of the Greek subaltern stationed there with his patrol, who wants them all for himself. As we give the peasants a fair price, they will gladly pass them to us secretly, and very good eggs they are.

30 June. Faith (O.C. our 3 Company detachment) temporarily sick, leaving me in command. Visit yesterday from Corps Commander (Lieut.-General Briggs), Divisional Commander (Major-General Longley) and our Brigadier Vandeleur.

4 July. Do not expect to be here much longer, it is too unhealthy a spot, and defences are well advanced. This morning rode right down the line : managed to pick up two okes of potatoes, one melon, chocolate biscuits, and some lettuce : of eggs a plentiful supply from the Greek post. The Greek officer in charge is a decent fellow. We have a tame jackdaw with us that will steal anything. Storks abound ; also cornflowers and other wild flowers, but the country is looking very parched ; except for an occasional thunderstorm, there will not be much more rain before October ; but this weather, though very hot, means much less discomfort than either cold or wet, and two bathes a day in a tepid river are not to be despised. The Struma flows two miles an hour.

25 July. Right down the Seres Road, at Adjvatli, working on the Derbend defences. Took four nights marching here.

1 Aug. Minden Day. Near Dremiglava. Whilst in hospital with fever have missed two exceptionally severe thunderstorms spent, I gather, in the middle of a ploughed field. The Hampshires have had a very bad time again on the Western Front. Am under a fig tree, with vines around.

6 Aug. A charming vineyard, except when a thunderstorm comes on ; an excellent village for vegetables and fruit near by. The C.O. is in excellent form, and Major Garsia who has been for long on the Staff, helping Serb Army recently, has joined as Second in Command. Hicks has applied for Flying Corps. Kit has to be carefully thought out ; reduced to 30 lbs. each officer, pack-mule transport being alone used. A big G.O.C.'s inspection yesterday, mainly of transport.

24 Aug. Am detached from main part of Battalion and, after a lot of night marching and counter-marching, back again under the fig tree. Faith is with me here. Shall soon know the main road to Seres intimately. The Bulgar is not tired of the war yet by a long way—why should he be ? After all he has still got Serbia.

27 Aug. Hope to ride over to Langaza one day soon. There are some hot baths there from natural springs.

29 Aug. Hicks and I having most peaceful time imaginable. On Sunday night, for instance, went to the village church and attended Greek service; highly instructive; were given seats of honour next " Papa " : Kyrie eleison (Lord have mercy) constantly repeated, and a prayer for King Constantine, were about all we understood. Afterwards a great competition to shake hands with us. A little dumbfoundered in the procession round the outside of the church, as the polite crowd pushed us up to the front. Yesterday a delightful ride westwards and back to camp through a lovely valley with bathing places made on the stream by our troops and lots of blackberries of the very best, and then a visit to the village festival, yesterday being a great feast day, where we saw the most beautiful dances, all in full local costume. There was one at Kirekeui last Easter, but this was far better stage-managed, and the background of wooden houses and sun setting behind the dancers all very striking. An old Turk provided music; he had a face just as one saw in Gallipoli, very dirty, very unshaven. To-day to Langaza, not so Greek as Dremiglava; plenty of Bulgars and Turks; it is on the lake of the same name.

30 Aug. Langaza a very cosmopolitan place. In addition to its ordinary fairly big population, full of refugees. Hotel Centrale gave a very good lunch. Dining room leads directly out of the very unsavoury stable, but such things are not noticed out here. Market place presented a very animated scene. Excellent news reached us last night, the entry of Roumania on side of Allies. Should make all the difference here. It will be interesting to see in what direction her first move will be. An advance on the left of the Russians would appear to open up disagreeable possibilities for the Bulgars. Hope one of the early results will be that Russian troops are allowed southwards through her territory. A jolly little tame lizard spends hours in my bivouac and eats flies.

3 Sept. The day before yesterday Faith and I rode into Salonika for the day, 18 kilos each way, but horses had four to five hours' rest in heat of the day and did journey well. Was fortunate enough to see something of another Salonika revolution—that of August 1916. It is true there was not much to see, a dead horse, and guns and trench mortars ready for action, and many French soldiers; but it was a very bloodless revolution. What the King will do now is the next matter of interest. The Macedonians appear to be all of one mind. A tiring and dusty day, but always interesting to see what new armies have arrived. Beginning to be quite difficult to know who is who. The Russians and Italians are both a fine looking lot of men. We were many different nations lunching at the Hotel Romain. At our table was a naval officer who had been through the Cameroons campaign with some naval guns. Yesterday Hicks and I practised the arts of peace and went out blackberrying. Last night, just after our return, came the worst wind and thunderstorm we have had. Bivouacs powerless to resist it. All is dry and sunny now. It is a great thing to have a big kit-bag into which all property will go when these storms come on.

7 Sept. Still passing a quiet time and usually have time to read the *Balkan News* (English), *L'Opinion* (French) and *Macedonia* (Greek) each day when I can get them. All Saints' Day, Greek Church, produced a very elaborate festival in neighbouring village, which Hicks and I attended as "delegates." "Johnny" is the villagers' method of introduction to his friends of any British soldiers, and the two Johnnies had to do much handshaking whilst we watched the dance in progress in the village square, all in the best native costumes. The most common boys' names seem to be Demetri, Vasseli, Georgios.

News good yesterday: Dar-es-Salaam fallen, continuance and progress of Somme offensive, and Russians progressing with the usual number of Austrian prisoners. Difficult to see how there can be any Austrian Army left if the figures given are correct. The Zeppelin raid, 13 strong, does not seem to have done much damage. We are fast getting to autumn now. Leave out of the question, though a month or two back a few officers with very strong reasons were getting a fortnight in England. Faith has given me the names of some of the birds and butterflies seen in this country. The small vulture, kite, kestrel and sparrow-hawk (as many as thirty kestrels are sometimes seen together), magpies without number, hoopoos, golden aureole, larks, swallows, house and sand martens, cuckoos. A few months ago there were many dragon flies, about five different colours at least. Lizards are very common, some over one foot in length, centipedes and snakes, both poisonous and non-poisonous. Of butterflies, large tortoiseshell and large copper, clouded yellow, silver-washed fritillary, purple hairstreak, white admirals, three or four different sorts of blues and skippers. Three sorts of swallowtails, meadow-browns, walls and heaths in great numbers, black-veined whites, green-veined whites.

9 Sept. In the Romani battle, Lancashire Infantry seem to have done very well, and as usual the Anzacs and Scotch Territorials.

10 Sept. Hicks and I discovered a local village schoolmaster who could speak French after a fashion, so we have hired him to come and teach us modern Greek each day. He is a refugee from Caesarea, Anatolia, and is quite useful.

13 Sept. Daily lessons in Greek have come to an untimely end, as his term has begun. His village is too far away for us to get over often. Accent, stress, and pronunciation are the main difficulties, and conversation is much more essential than bookwork. Went for a walk with the troops and mules through the most lovely country yesterday—gorges, streams, woods and mountains. Hicks has just heard he has been accepted as an Observer in R.F.C. He will not be many miles away, but I do not expect I shall see much more of him.

14 Sept. Two severe blows have fallen simultaneously. Faith is off to be Camp Commandant on Lines of Communication with rank of a Major : a good job for him and well deserved. Hicks has left to-day to be attached to R.F.C. as an Observer. Have done all my riding and walking and expeditions and a lot of work with one or other of them, and already feel their loss very much. Shall probably be off soon and away from vineyard for good and in for a more active life.

24 Sept. Days are pretty busy now training and getting drafts ready in addition also to being my own Adjutant and C.O. Men back from hospital and direct from England put in as much work here as they can, before proceeding further up country. Scarcely ever get out of the vineyard now.

The Battalion has been in one fight [Battle of Karadzakoi Zir and Bala (30 Sept. - 4 Oct.)]. Very light casualties, though one officer killed, the only officer hit. Serbs and Franco - Russians on the left are undoubtedly doing well.

7 Oct. Am still in the vineyard, though about 300 yards away from my late bivouac, and in a very comfortable bell tent left me by the Colonel of the Connaught Rangers. We have any amount of sheds about, wood and corrugated iron, so those who are left are settling in comfortably. I am now O.C. all the Brigade details. Brigade detailed me for the job, but I am in hopes that when all the mules are wanted at the front they will release me from here. I have three officers in charge of their surplus regimental mules, and some 200 mules, but very few men to look after them, too few, and we are rather hard put to it.

Am scarcely in touch with the outside world, my only line of communication being my groom, whom I send up once a day to a telegraph station up the line about 5 kilos away. Faith lives near there, and I shall try and get over and see him sometimes ; also a despatch-rider occasionally comes with orders ; otherwise no one takes any notice of me. Each mule costs about £80 by the time it arrives at Salonika from Mexico, etc. Fortunately they have left behind a good A.V.C. sergeant. All I can do is to see the place is kept clean and that the mules are properly fed and groomed. Except for my Hampshire men, the rest are all Irish.

11 Oct. I am having dumps in the neighbourhood cleared up, and all the material we do not want ourselves returned to R.E. or Ordnance. The mules give very little trouble and are being well looked after. News is scanty. I live on an occasional *Balkan News* and rumours from Major Faith. We have had to shoot a lot of pariah dogs which infest the camp at night and walk off with all the food if they are allowed. Salonika does not hold out many attractions, though I shall probably have to go in again one day soon. Progress in France seems steady. I follow every move possible on my large collection of maps.

15 Oct. No doubt we have some bad weather to come, but it is hotter here to-day than midsummer at home. The leaves are fast falling off the trees in the vineyard; otherwise there is little to show that autumn has come. Sending telegrams and indenting for forage are the main excitements of the day.

18 Oct. I see from *Punch* John Masefield has written a book on Gallipoli; also Creighton. He was Chaplain, 86th Brigade, and we were 88th; so I expect he has a lot to say about the " incomparable 29th," which is a new Division now to all intents and purposes. I remember vividly Col. Beckwith and myself talking to him one evening on W Beach the night before we went into the front line.

Hicks came down to earth the other day, but is none the worse; fortunately just in our lines.

22 Oct. Am splashing about in transport lines and sending off various details of men and mules. One of the biggest thunderstorms I have ever seen visited us last night, and the whole camp is worse than a ploughed field and with the greatest difficulty one can move about at all. I expect to get orders to move my Brigade details up the line any day now, 50 kilos or so, to join Battalion. Faith has got his motor at last, a very nice car; he took me up the line to a place I wanted to go to yesterday.

28 Oct. The worst part of the journey is over, as I have now arrived at Divisional H.Q. with my party of pilgrims—a real circus we have looked like during the 50 kilos that we have journeyed. My party consisted mainly of old men who did not know one end of a mule from the other: they had to ride one mule and lead one or two others. One old military policeman had to be heaved on to his mule after each halt. The three G.S. wagons that accompanied us required teams of eight to get them up some of the hills and out of the mud: there was one day of heavy rain which churned up everything. The first day I absolutely failed to get to the kilo that I was ordered to, but Faith kindly took over ammunition and bombs for me and I was able to make it up next day. We are all resting now in the intervals of watering and feeding mules: the watering-place is down a precipice. To-morrow morning I ride on to Brigade for orders, and shall gladly hand all over to their regiments and return to the Battalion.

I saw the Colonel in a C.C. Station on the way up. He was able to tell me a good deal of first-hand news. He tells me the trenches at the bridge-head were used by our forces in the attack, but they will be full of water by now.

29 Oct. Arrived at last and reported to Brigade H.Q. Am at present with the Battalion transport, and shall probably ride up this afternoon to our village, where I am told all is quite peaceful at present. Find I am receiving Major's pay as Second in Command, which is satisfactory. Not as much damage has been done to the charming village near which I am sitting as I expected. Shall be living at H.Q. for the time being, till the Colonel comes back. We are at present in front line trenches, but the Bulgars are a long way away, though our patrols sometimes come into contact with them.

30 Oct. Have operation orders to study for a new show in which our job will be a very easy one, as the 29th Brigade have had some nasty jobs lately. Slept in a dug-out last night but it is too musty, and I am going into a tent which I managed to bring up the line. At present it is being well concealed in brushwood from aeroplanes which occasionally come over.

1 Nov. Very busy yesterday : there was fighting most of day on our front, but 10th Hampshires came off lightly. 28th Division attacked at Barakli Dzuma, and the 10th Division Prosenik and Patrol Wood, about 2,000 yards from Kalendra. 10th Hampshires in reserve, but on withdrawal of attacking troops we occupied Kalendra Wood, finding advanced posts along the railway. Very comfortable in the village. Battalion are out doing outpost duty. Davies and I will be riding out to see them soon : they have had a very quiet night I fancy. The Bulgars (or Germans) know how to use their guns : they gave our woods a lot of shelling yesterday.

No sooner had the C.O. and I arrived at the wood than about thirty shells (only five casualties, all wounded) came in and around it. One landed where five officers, including our two selves, had been talking three minutes before. There were a lot of mules trenched round the wood at the time, and this must have drawn the attention of their gunners. Another sailed over just as we were mounting to move on and burst twenty yards away. Just got a message through that we are moving off to the right early to-morrow and our outposts are being taken over by another regiment to-night.

3 Nov. 10th Hampshires transferred from 29th Brigade, 10th Division, to 82nd Brigade, 27th Division, and we moved to Karadzakoi. We are in our new quarters and have changed our Brigade and Division. The new Staff, both Divisional and Brigade, seem pleasant, and both Generals gave us a very hearty welcome yesterday. My new house is a very pleasant dug-out in a fairly well-known village where we now have Battalion H.Q. I shall be going round our new trenches more thoroughly this afternoon. It is a very safe part of the line, no Bulgars near. The village church is almost intact, except for one shell-hole, and we shall have Church Parade there on Sundays. Meanwhile the village is in our charge. When we have got it cleaned up I do not think it will be a bad place, though it promises to be rather a damp part of the line later, and some of the dug-outs on the river bank are untenable.

5 Nov. We are going to move again. Fortunately it is not a long move, and then I think we shall be allowed to settle down and make some sort of winter quarters for the men. We shall miss our village for H.Q., but I fancy one of the Companies may get another village for their H.Q. Yesterday I rode over to the Divisional Canteen to try and get some sort of a canteen for the Battalion. There are wild rumours of leave during the winter, but such rumours have never ceased since I arrived out here. Plenty of melons, marrows and mushrooms about, so we do not do so badly. Generals Sarrail and Rocques were about in this neighbourhood yesterday, but I saw nothing of them.

6 Nov. Took over trenches on right of and across Komarjan Bridge.

8 Nov. We have now moved to the place where I rather hope we shall be allowed to make some kind of winter quarters. A lot of us ordered some bivouacs (32s., and weighing 1 lb. 12 oz.) from England some time ago. They have come and are very satisfactory. We may get bell tents soon which will be more comfortable for the men, for if we get really wet weather and the river rises it will be no joke here. Roumanian news is a bit better nowadays. It looks as if they wanted to get hold of their Transylvania rather too quickly. Whatever the " encircling battle of Hermanstadt " may have really been it was a nasty smack in the eye for Roumania. Perhaps now that Russia seems to have taken over the Dobrudja the Roumanians will have better fortune on their northern frontier.

9 Nov. I have to ride over to a village this morning about getting a Battalion canteen started. This afternoon Col. Beckett returns, so I expect I move house once more. We have been in the new Division about a week, and it will be about my fourth move.

10 Nov. A half-Company relieved Gloucesters at Agomah.

12 Nov. I have had two days riding since the C.O. came back going round all new positions with him. During this week I hope to get back to my Company. Heard from Hicks yesterday. He tells me he was up above us when we were shelled in that wood the other day, and was trying to get our guns on to the Bulgar battery. We rather miss our friends in the old Brigade, but as far as we can tell in these early days we shall quite like ourselves here. Two Bulgars spent last night with us, taken out in front. Their one desire was sleep, and they seemed not unhappy that their soldiering career was over for a time. I saw a wonderful Bulgar shell-hole yesterday, about the biggest I have seen. I think the shell must have come from Rupel during the battle for Bala and Zir.

15 Nov. Battalion re-formed into four Companies.

18 Nov. At Osman Kamilla. We have been on the move since Tuesday, and though we personally have not had any serious fighting, yet we have got our share of shells. At 11 p.m. on 16th we moved to Pheasant Wood preparatory to attack on Tumbitza Farm.

20 Nov. At Jenimah. At last we have got a good night's rest, for we marched back into reserve after dark last night, and are now in a very good house with fine stable complete, and some of our transport has joined us. Yesterday afternoon the news reached us of the fall of Monastir, and it looks as if we have had our share in it as we have been doing perpetual demonstrations for five days and must have prevented the Bulgars from moving away any troops, and possibly caused them to bring more. I had a two-night job of holding two villages, Salmah and Kispeki, and a longish line between with a not too strong Company. However, in spite of various messages of threatening Bulgar counter-attacks, nothing happened. About 1 a.m. I got a Vickers gun into the line in addition to the two Company Lewis guns, and after that we had a greater feeling of security : all the same I was thankful when dawn came and we could see where we were, for we did not get into the new line till darkness had fallen, and a digging party of another regiment that Brigade sent off lost their way and did not get started till an hour after dawn, so a part of the line was only patrolled for the best part of the night. Possibly, however, the Bulgars are not feeling very aggressive after the gruelling they got at Bala ; I have been told that 2,000 dead were counted on the wire in front alone ; and that 5,000 killed is the estimated total on one part of the line. The Bulgars evidently had no idea our R.E. could have got the wire out so quickly, and they counter-attacked with great bravery. A Greek battalion is attached to our Brigade. The C.O. has sent in my name for Second in Command.

21 Nov. Yesterday we went round the line held by the Greek battalion. If only I had not had 10 miles to walk I should have enjoyed it more. Expect we shall take over from the Greeks some day.

26 Nov. At Jenimah. Still at the same place and in the same billets. Life is quiet and normal again though there is plenty of digging, patrols, and other routine work to be done. Chase is away in hospital sick, and Harfield is doing acting Adjutant, so we are a bit shorthanded in the Company: however the platoon sergeants are efficient. I have now a Bulgar pony attached to me; my groom found him, and he is very useful for carrying extra kit, and am now going out on him to visit some piquets I have out in front. All is very quiet, and it is not an afternoon for the " tin hat " which we all possess now. Some rather nice chrysanthemums growing outside, also very good mushrooms in the neighbourhood which we enjoy at breakfast. We have heard the bare news that the *Britannic* and *Braemar Castle* have been lost. Another man of X Company at Cape Helles has turned up here. He got the D.C.M. for good work on the Peninsula, and reminded me that he was one of the bombing party the day I was hit.

28 Nov. We have had a long day making and improving a new track for transport from one of the new bridges over the river. A Coy. is quite strong again, a very pleasant experience. " Josey " was in great form to-day. It has been perfect weather the last few days, beautifully sunny and not too warm, and I much enjoyed finding out the tracks and nearest course for the road to take. Some gunners also gave us a very good lunch. An odd coincidence that Serbs should have taken Monastir exactly four years to the day since they took it from the Turks in 1912, November 19th. General Sarrail, in an order issued to the Allied Armies, refers to the British Army, " Yours has been a thankless task," etc., and then follows an eulogy of how cheerfully, etc., etc., it has been carried out.

2 Dec. There was a good deal of fighting round this neighbourhood in May 1913, just before outbreak of Second Balkan War, and the Bulgars were quietly occupying parts of Macedonia that both they and the Greeks wanted. I was one of a party who rode over to the Greek lines to do an Entente call (Brigade Orders); however, as they were being shelled at the time, we decided that they would have no use for callers, and came home again. Lieut.-Colonel Doughty Wylie, V.C., who was killed above V Beach, was a Wykehamist. It was he and Williams of the Hampshires that did great doings near V Beach just after the landing.

7 Dec. Verhanli and Tumbitza. We are still on very active service and have not yet got the job done which we set out to do on Monday night. Tuesday afternoon I took out one of my platoons on a reconnaissance in force to find out information about a bridge over a stream, and various other things. The C.O. is in command of one group, which includes the Greeks. I shall be working on their left to-morrow with my Company. Carruthers is the only one of my original officers with me at the moment, but he is invaluable. We have with us now only the kit we can carry into action, the rest is back at our late billets ; but we are getting up the dixies to-night, so ought to get a drop of hot tea for breakfast to-morrow. Beyond the fact that we cannot cook, owing to the smoke being too great an attraction for the Bulgar gunners to resist, rations have been excellent. Last night there were three bombardments, each lasting about 10 minutes, doing a barrage for some troops who had to withdraw from a wood, and I only woke up for the first minute or two. All the hills opposite were lit up with the bursting shells.

10 Dec. It is all over. We have been back two days now in a little house where we only get shelled. The Company are in trenches round the village, Company H.Q. in the little house which we have frequently had to evacuate for funk-holes outside. What a night of digging we had, driving rain and bitterly cold, but we had our reward in the morning when they shelled the village and a battery of field guns in my line. A Gunner corporal had his head taken off. I had a shell right in one of my platoon trenches, but fortunately it was in a traverse where no one was. My Company have had no casualties from shell-fire since we did the reconnaissance in force, when one of my orderlies was hit by our own guns just before I had sent up Verey lights ordering them to lift from the village on the bluffs. They lifted as though by magic immediately the two white lights went up and fairly doused the bluffs, so that not a Bulgar shewed his head whilst we investigated the village. My total find of living creatures was one dog. I never had to take the bluff which was to have been my job, connecting up with the Greeks on my right who were creeping through the village first. We should have got the bluff all right, but I doubt if we should have held it after dawn. " The Bluff " was a steep sandstone cliff with two trenches at least halfway up and an observation post on the top. I think we should have gone up without difficulty, as the guns were going to give us a big barrage, but it all rather depended on what Monsieur le Commandant and his crowd did. Events are rather confused in my mind ; nights and days are blurred into one, and it is hard to realize only a week has passed since we left our late comfortable but flea-haunted billets. It is now after 7 p.m., and I am sitting over a wood fire whilst my servant is brewing Ivelcon in a tin for myself and to send out to my Platoon Commanders in the trenches just in front. All is ready to move at a moment's notice, and back we go during the night to what will I am sure prove a more healthy spot.

A German 'plane dropped three bombs on us yesterday searching for the battery which, much to our delight, had departed during the night, as we were getting rather tired of the shells that were meant for them.

Many vague rumours are floating about, but as I have not seen a paper for a week I do not credit them all. I am inclined to believe

Bucharest has fallen, but I doubt whether Lloyd George and Mr. Asquith have both resigned, also that we are in a state of war with the King and Royalist party. Fortunately my groom has been able to bring up "Josey" to-night, who is tethered outside contentedly munching straw. As we have a longish night march, I shall be very thankful for her company.

12 Dec. Suhabanja. After a long and exhaustive march [from Beklik Mah] we got into our new billets in quite a charming village. A Company have particularly nice billets, nearly all with fireplaces and quite well built and not like where we have been during operations, where a mud hut was a luxury.

15 Dec. We seem to have settled down again. There is little to trouble us here except enemy aeroplanes, and their visits are not very frequent. Our quarters are not too bad either, though for preference I still keep in my bivouac which is pitched alongside the house. The mountains in the far distance are capped with snow, and even the nearer ones occasionally have a white coat in the morning, but down here in the plain by day it is warm, just comfortably so, though cold and frosty at night. It is jolly country for riding, and I get out most days to visit posts—or at any rate try and find some excuse. "Josey" is in fine fettle and requires plenty of exercise.

17 Dec. We hear by wireless to-day Greece has given in to all our demands. It was hardly expected we should still be at peace with her after the last ultimatum. Our Greek Nationalist army has moved off elsewhere. Masefield's *Gallipoli* is excellent, particularly where he lets himself go, and does not describe the bare facts.

23 Dec. With Christmas Day on Monday, we have so far got in only a quarter of the canteen stores that we have ordered and ought to have. All this is due to the shocking state in which the road is, our main, in fact our only line of communication. However things are looking up and the prospects are distinctly more cheering this afternoon. It is odd, but it just shows that the valley is the place to be in now from the point of view of comfort. Behind us perpetual rain up in the hills, in front of us snow, Bulgars, and for aught I know other horrors. So really we who are basking in the sun this afternoon are very well off. The C.O. got a mention in the recent despatch, *Times*, Dec. 7, I believe it was. Division have granted me four days' leave in Salonika, so I shall shortly decamp to the best hotel, the best dinner, the best cigars, the best baths, the best white sheets that Salonika can produce. Am sending home a Greek service book which I found in an abandoned church. I do not think we shall get to Athens after all, though there might still be a chance. *The History of the Balkans* (Arnold Toynbee, Hogarth, etc.) is quite first-rate.

28 Dec. Yesterday we did a rapid move of our billets from one part of the village to another part. Taken over B Company's, which were better. I have also got a jolly room to myself with a good view.

Have not yet gone off on my four days' leave. Am starting first nine miles on " Josey," 5 a.m. on Saturday morning, and shall pick up motor convoy at 8 a.m. on the road. With luck ought to get right down same night. If not shall put up with Faith on the way.

We had quite a nice Christmas Day. Service in the village church at 9.30, and a football match, Officers v. Sergeants, in the afternoon.

Masefield's descriptive parts of the scenery of the Peninsula, Lemnos, with the peak of Samothrace in the distance, are very good. Also the fighting in the vineyard before Krithia. I lent it to the man who was with me on the bombing raid, and he read and apparently enjoyed it all.

We have old friends (Turks) opposite to us now, some way away it is true. The others (Bulgars) I suppose have gone round to Monastir. Hicks is now at Salonika. He expected to be sent off to thwart schemes in Thessaly, but nothing seems to have come of it yet.

1917.

4 Jan. My short leave is over, and highly successful it has been. I got back soon after 5 o'clock this evening. The journey started on Saturday last at 5.30, when " Josey," my groom, servant and I crawled nine miles in the dark to the main road to catch the 8 a.m. convoy. That took me about 10 miles, and then I was fortunate enough to pick up two cars in succession which landed me at Faith's rest camp about 12 noon. There I lunched, and went quietly in during the afternoon by lorry, only 25 kilos this last part. I eventually, after a few enquiries, booked a room at the Hotel Splendide, the best hotel as it turned out. My servant also got a nice little niche with a bed in it. The first day and a half were spent doing shopping commissions.

Most of the members of the Provisional Government live at Hotel Splendide, and I now can number amongst my distant acquaintances Admiral Condouriotis (Navy), Gen. Danglis (War), Nigroponti (Finance) and the late A.D.C. to King Constantine. Venizelos was in on New Year's Eve; unfortunately I had just gone to bed and missed him. He was very pleased as he had just got news of Lord Granville's appointment as Agent to him from Great Britain. I lunched at the famous Floca's café, a great place for meeting officers of all the Allied nations. Everyone can speak some sort of French, varying from the best Parisian to the worst Serb, Italian and Montenegrian accents. I lunched one day with A.D.C. to Serb General of Danube Division : thought he was French till halfway through, when he apologized for his bad French, and I was feeling a little surprised that we understood each other so well. He explained he was a Serb ; mutual confusion and apologies. And then another day I discussed the Carso with two Italian subaltern Gunners just come from there. Another day I had the experiences of a Montenegrian. Every Greek in Salonika seems to like the British forces now, though most admit they were received at first " avec froideur," whilst it was all " Vive la France." An evening at the Tour Blanche was amusing. Yesterday midday I started back, and spent last night with Faith : started again at 8 a.m. After a few miles picked up R.F.C. tender which was bound for Hicks' detachment ; arrived there to see Hicks just leaving aerodrome for a one and a half hour's reconnaissance, and awaited his return. Meanwhile a wire came in to say we had brought down a German 'plane near by. The victorious pilot arrived back to lunch. They always let the Germans know result of an air contest, so following was made out in triplicate and put in specially made bags : " Your aeroplane No. — brought down behind our lines—Pilot slightly wounded—Observer unhurt, receiving every attention, signed R.F.C." Then a pilot (this all took place at lunch) was detailed to drop the three messages—and the victor, next to whom I was sitting, said would I like to go over with him ? So at 2.45 p.m., Jan. 4, 1917, I " took the air " for the first time. It was a most interesting experience ; we went over all the well-known (to me) places, and also the unknown (to me) town of Seres, where we dropped two of the messages on the barracks. Finally I was landed not five kilos from where " Josey " was waiting to bring me home.

14 Jan. Agomah. We are leaving our village to-morrow for three weeks. A big draft has turned up and two more officers for my Company, Jago and Playford by name. Have now got four platoon commanders : No. 1, Jago ; No. 2, Carruthers (the best and most capable officer) ; No. 3, Playford ; No. 4, Howe.

21 Jan. It is Tuesday morning, and a cold one at that. Yesterday was bitterly cold and this morning on waking up we saw many more hills with snow on them, both our own hills behind and also the Bulgar hills in front. My present cottage is made of mud, and is horribly draughty, but we may move again any day to search for another spot to lie up for Turkish patrols. One of our three weeks is already up. However Division and Brigade both seem to be pleased with the small stirring up of the Turk that we have been able to do.

25 Jan. It has continued snowing pretty well all day. We had made arrangements to leave our village to-night on four days' operations, but Division cancelled them an hour or so ago. A Company had all the front to hold as an outpost line that we reconnoitred on Monday ; I should have been the only lucky Company with a village for Company

H.Q. Even Battalion H.Q. were to live in bivouacs in a wood. I had about four fords to hold and various places to patrol. Perhaps when the weather gets better and the authorities have no occasion to fear frost-bites and trench feet for the men it will come off. Yesterday the Divisional Follies visited us, and with Divisional Band gave us a very good show lasting two hours—the first amusement the men have had since many months ago. We are all enjoying *The Uncensored Letters from the Dardanelles*. Henry Bell, an Old Wykehamist and Captain in the Surrey Yeomanry, did a cavalry reconnaissance the other day at the fords. Later we got fired on by a Turkish scout, no one hurt and they soon cleared off. Unfortunately we had no chance of rounding them up, as I was out with platoon officers and sergeants and only about six men. We managed to see everything we wanted to without opposition. These mealy fields are very difficult, and the Turk is clever at lying doggo whilst the cavalry look round, and then is ready for the infantry patrols. Hicks tells me on high Corps authority that the 10th Hampshires have already made a great name for efficiency in their new Brigade.

26 Jan. The weather put a stop to our proposed activity : instead we are staying on at our mud-hut village. It has been snowing and raining again to-day, chiefly the latter, and you can picture the state of mud everything is in. A journey to Battalion H.Q., which are in reality a few minutes away, constitutes quite a walk. Wood for fires is getting scarce, and this morning I demolished a barn attached to my house : my house is still standing. I see the Doctor found the ruins of Pella near Alakilise, which is a village considerably nearer Topsin, where the French lived after the retreat from Serbia last winter, than Yenidze - Vardar, a dirty Turkish village, which I had understood was the site of ancient Pella. It has not the appearance of a suitable place for Philip of Macedonia's H.Q., nor a particularly charming place for Alexander to have been born at. When the poor inhabitants return here, they will find a great scarcity of building materials. The little houses are miserable things at the best, but there is generally one decent white-washed two-storied house in each village. The poor horses and mules have a bad time this cold weather, but I am glad to say they all have rugs now. There was a good deal of gun-fire last night, but we were not turned out.

28 Jan. The water is so inadequate here that I took the Company down to the Struma this afternoon so that they could get some necessary washing of clothes, and of themselves, done. The snow has disappeared from the valley again, but still plenty of mud about.

6 Feb. We are off to-morrow to Kispeki Wood. This is to be an A Company show.

14 Feb. Apidje. Now we are back in rest billets again, I with my Company detached (H.Q. and three Companies at Suhabanja), about a mile and a half away from Battalion H.Q. in quite a good village, though it is rather a wet and muddy one. I even have a house to myself.

18 Feb. The little village we are billeted in at present is very typical of the best villages out here. The inevitable white house with smaller houses clustered round it and poplars and willows, also a very pretty stream with a rustic bridge in addition to a business-like bridge which our R.E. have put up. We are again back and working at roads near Gudeli Bridge, and only hear the murmur of the guns in the distance. The Battalion that relieved us has had better luck than we had, probably due to the fact that now the snow has gone the Turk is moving from his camp fires. He was a wise man not to lie out when we did. My Company are on detachment here, and the Colonel, who has just paid us a visit, was quite pleased with a bath house, hot water at half an hour's notice, we have fitted up. The Band of the Middlesex Regiment are coming to play to us to-night. I have a very nice copper tea tray which I must try and send home some time : my servant found it ; it is a very nice piece. "Josey" took me down to the river this morning, where the men are working, and it was altogether delightful with the sun out, and all the mud drying up and disappearing, and a spring feeling in the air.

21 Feb. I went for a very nice ride down Tahinos Lake to Fitoki and Barakta Mah on Monday with the M.O., partly on business, partly a joy-ride. On the way I had my ear pricked by a bacteriologist, and the blood smeared on a slide ; something to do with malaria tests or statistics. I am just off to Brigade canteen to try and get some green peas to go with two ducks that the C.O. shot and presented me with. I have not been out with him lately, as I am on detachment and more than a mile away.

2 Mar. I have been away two days on a Gas Course at Divisional Headquarters. All Company Commanders and C.O.'s are going. We lived in tents, and I am glad to be back in a comfortable billet. *Land and Water* rather cracks us up now and says we " paralyze the Central Empires in the East."

4 Mar. We are still back, and I went for a ride this afternoon over to our old Division at Mekes to see if I could find anyone about, but our old Brigade has left and gone up, so I turned the ride into an instructive one and learned some more about the country. One never knows when one may have to walk the Company or Battalion somewhere or other on a pitch-black night, and that is not an easy job, especially in Macedonia where the so-called roads, really tracks, look much alike and only differ in the amount of mud and flowing steams. The book from which to learn Geography is Arnold Toynbee's *Nationality and the War*: it is a most suggestive book and delightful reading. One of my platoon sergeants has to-day got a Commission in the Hampshire Regiment and in this Battalion, so he has just gone off to another Company. He should make a good officer.

7 Mar. Just come home from a very nice hot bath in my washhouse in this village. Our month will be up next Thursday, and I expect we shall move up again. This is a very jolly village at this time of year, and the Company will be sorry to leave it. I attended a very good lecture yesterday at Division by General Weir, who has just come back from a fortnight with Gough and the Vth Army. All the latest; truly marvellous what we have learned by experience. Hicks hopes in about a month to go off to learn the pilot's job, at the same time get a little leave which he is thinking of spending in Italy. I should love to go with him, but it is quite impossible. Fortunately I have got leave to cut down certain trees in this village, so we have been well off for fuel, even down to fires in billets, and fuel for the wash-house.

12 Mar. Yesterday I was out riding round a new piece of the line near Osman Kamila that we are going to take over shortly. It is wonderfully interesting out here I find, and I rarely suffer from the common complaint of boredom. My name has been sent in by Brigade to command a Labour Battalion, but as I do not answer to any of the disqualifications required, I sincerely hope I shall not get it. It would not necessarily mean promotion, and I prefer the 10th Hampshires.

Easter Day, **8 April.** Osman Kamila. We shall have helmets issued any day now; it is warming up fast. Storks are building all over the village, and the fruit trees are full of blossom; a particularly fine pear tree just outside our mess. Everything is very green and spring-like, but in a month or two the sun will turn the green grass brown. I am not looking forward to another Macedonian summer.

12 Apr. They have given me a Majority. I am glad to say it does not mean leaving A Company, as Major Davies is still here as Second in Command. We are having a rather more strenuous week out of the line than in it. Hours 8.30 - 11.30, and 4 - 7. I have heard no more about commanding a Labour Battalion, so hope that is off.

25 Apr. Second Anniversary of Landing at Helles. Two years ago to-day at dawn the Landing at Helles took place.

3 May. Hot weather and mosquitoes are with us. Another week or so of this delightful village (Osman Kamila) and then I expect we shall move. Bennett (recently from C Company) and Carruthers and myself are doing all the Company work at present, as my other officers are either understudying Adjutants or looking after canteens.

8 May. A hot and sultry day ending in a thunderstorm. Carruthers is back from leave, so stress of work has eased off somewhat. I have just finished a rather entertaining French book, *En Macedonie*, all about the retreat from Serbia, November and December 1915, by a French sergeant with a distinct sense of humour. The wild flowers are a wonderful sight, especially the poppies and daisies. There are literally acres of red and white; also on the Bulgar side one can see great patches of colour, enormous pure white poppies and mauve ones of about the same size flourish in abundance. We are going to try young nettles in the place of vegetables, which are a bit scarce. The daily sick report is surprisingly low for the time of year, but then we learned a good many lessons last summer, both regimental officers and M.O.'s.

18 May. We have not moved yet, though our dump containing what we cannot carry on pack transport has been shifted. A Divisional vegetable garden which has been started is a great success : we get plenty of lettuces and other green food from it.

20 May. I rode over to a village called Kispeki this morning on business. Last time I was there snow was on the ground; now it is more like a jungle, wild flowers and insects in profusion. I shall probably be going out there again to-night.

27 May. The Salonika Army has started a great economy campaign; amongst other things it is not the thing to be seen walking about in brand new clothing and equipment : the more you are covered with patches (trousers, jackets, shorts and elsewhere) the better. The question of shipping supplies to us is evidently giving trouble at home, and before many months are past we shall in many respects be self-supporting, as we shall be manufacturing soap, cultivating vegetable gardens, and catching fish. Thunderstorms are becoming fairly frequent. They go right along both sides of the valley, and occasionally, if we are lucky, we miss them, but though everyone may get soaked they are dry again a few hours afterwards and really we have very little to complain of.

4 June. Last night appointed as Second in Command of our 12th Battalion, and as their C.O. has recently become a casualty shall probably find myself commanding. I do not want to leave these nice people, especially the C.O. here, one little bit; but as it had to be I am glad it is to the Hampshires. I shall be handing over here to-day, stay a night with Faith, who has a car and will help me to do some necessary shopping, and then after a day or two catch the train that runs up in the direction of Lake Doiran. I fancy I shall find the Brigade very much cut up; they had a bad time recently. They are in a quiet place at present reorganizing. Anyhow it is a new front.

5 June. I left the Battalion at 4 a.m. and arrived at Faith's camp about 10 o'clock, being very fortunate in getting a car nearly all the way with only a few miles of lorry. It was horrible leaving everyone, both officers and the Company. The C.O. was delightful and did all he could to prevent my going, but in vain. The best subaltern in the Battalion, one Griffith, has taken over A Company, and I know it is in good hands. Faith now dines and sleeps at advanced G.H.Q. near by, and I shall be with him to-night and to-morrow. I have the loan of Faith's car to-morrow and shall spend four or five hours shopping in Salonika, and then off from the new Struma front railhead near by at 5 o'clock on Thursday, in a supply train drawn by a L. & S.W. engine across country to junction for Doiran Line, and so on to Doiran front railhead. So has closed twelve months almost to a day on the Struma front, and in two days time I shall be beginning to become acquainted with the Doiran front. The Struma Valley has been a great experience, and I shall always remember, on the whole, the most pleasant time I have spent there. It will take many years to erase all the digging the 10th Hampshires have done there. I reported by telephone to the Base Camp whither I am supposed to be bound, and have thus avoided it, and this afternoon I have booked up a cattle truck with the R.T.O. After consulting a map, I discovered how at any rate to begin looking for my new Battalion.

8 June, near Mackukovo, " M " Sector, east of River Vardar. After various wanderings I arrived late last night at my new front. We are in a quiet part of the line, and going back in a day or two. I have just been in a train, the first time since I left Egypt.

10 June. The acting C.O. (the proper C.O. was wounded recently) is a Hampshire-Argyll and Sutherlander who has also been an East Lancs. and Welch Fusilier. He beats my record hollow—I have been with six different battalions since the War began and as many divisions —but it has been my good luck that they were all Hampshire battalions. We go back from front line on left bank of Vardar to-night into divisional reserve. The country is beautiful and a change from the Struma Valley. Am also interested in seeing an entirely different part of the Balkans. Went round our line last night with the C.O. It is tremendously up hill and down dale.

14 June. I like the Colonel immensely—Lindsey is his name: he is the ideal of an Indian Army officer, no fuss, very level-headed and very thorough. He was in command of a Territorial battalion which was almost next door to us at Helles. A lovely view from my tent high up on the spur of a hill, on the banks of the Vardar River which one sees winding its way to the next hills and the sea. I get at least one long ride a week, as I have to go to railhead (Karasouli) to see about canteen stores for the Battalion. The French are next door to us, over the river.

17 June. Lovely country, and I am sure much healthier than the Struma Valley. I have only just met the new Brigadier and do not know much about the Brigade yet. A good Devon battalion does time in and out of the line with us. We have just had news of the last big air raid over East London, and of King Constantine's departure.

21 June. I rode down to railhead (Karasouli) again yesterday; the heat was intense, and I was glad to get back to our comparatively breezy camp. We move shortly for a week in the line, then out again for a fortnight. The flowers are even better here than in the Struma Valley, and quite good little greengages and mulberries. One can realise better here what the retreat from Serbia must have been like in the winter of 1915, no roads, but rocky mountains in abundance.

26 June. Our hill camp, on spur overlooking River Vardar, is cool compared with what it is down below; to-morrow we move up into the line and dug-outs for a week. Lots of aerial activity here.

28 June. The C.-in-C. (General Milne) has been round to visit us in the front line this morning.

1 July. We shall be going out of the line on Tuesday night, and shall get a fortnight's training. We are trying nightly to catch a Saxon, but have not caught one yet, though we have great-coats as evidence of who is opposite to us.

6 July. Gully Ridge. We spent Tuesday and Wednesday night being relieved and marching back, and a Vardar wind blew hard for two days, and made everything practically impossible. We gained some credit for getting back a Lewis gun and magazines which had been lost by another regiment. A wire has just arrived necessitating my going over to the Struma front again on Monday. I shall be training in from railhead here Sunday night and a car from my late Division will meet me in Salonika and take me up; probably be away at least five days. Colonel Beckett has got a Brevet Lieut.-Colonelcy.

15 July. East of Vardar River opposite Mackukovo. Sunday midnight I went off to the Struma. A Divisional car met me in Salonika and took me right up to the Battalion at Nigoslav Camp. There I had to give evidence at a court of enquiry on an officer who had been missing for some weeks; a Bulgar deserter, also present, brought in clear evidence that he was a prisoner and safe in Philippopolis. The regimental commander before whom he was taken gave him twenty francs, as he had only two francs on him. It was a most curious case. The Bulgars are without doubt the best of the Balkan peoples, Greeks not excepted, and it is a thousand pities that we are on opposite sides. I returned to Salonika after visiting my late Company, who were in the line, and after a night at the Splendide returned here on Thursday, since when I have had to conduct two courts-martial. Last night a lecture at Brigade, and now I am in charge of Military and Recreational Training for the summer months, and am immersed in committees, sub-committees and documents. Tuesday we start off for the line. I shall be riding over this afternoon to see what we have got to take over, as it is a new bit of the line to all of us. The Russian offensive is cheering, and Brusiloff is the right man in the right place evidently.

22 July. We are compelled to sleep and work at odd times, the latter from 4 to 7 or 8 a.m. and then from 5 p.m. or so onwards till any hour. It is quite impossible to get about in the middle of the day, and unless one has a cool dug-out and good net as protection from the flies it is difficult to sleep during the day. This is a low-lying sector and the mosquitoes are bad, but by dint of starting extensive grass fires we are improving matters a good deal. The Bulgars doing the same, as we neither of us want a grass fire started by the opposing side, which frequently happens when shells are about. I am reading Harry de Windt's book, *Through Savage Europe*; it is enlightening on the Balkans and bears out the general opinion of the Bulgars.

29 July. We are naturally interested in the Paris Conference of last week. Personally I do not mind whether we stay here or go elsewhere. Colonel Beckett (10th) is probably being transferred to another theatre of war, and his second in command has just been given command of an East Lancashire battalion over this way: all this reconciles me a good deal to any move; everyone is changing in the 10th Battalion, and Carruthers has gone to look after troops at Corfu. Brigade Staff are a very pleasant lot, which all helps to make life agreeable.

3 Aug. We came out of the line Wednesday night after having, particularly one Company, a pretty heavy shelling for two days. The Bulgars eventually raided one of our works two hours after we had been relieved, but the guns got into them very promptly, and it was a dismal failure. We had one piece of real bad luck. An enemy shell (they were shooting at one of the aeroplanes spotting for our guns) fell in our H.Q. and exploded on the ground; most of the guard were knocked out, otherwise our casualties whilst in the line were small. It is remarkable how many hundred shells it takes to kill a man: 250 one day and one man very slightly wounded.

6 Aug. The guns gave somewhat of a display on the 4th, just to show the war had lasted three years. Leave has started again.

12 Aug. I played football again last night, first time since Boxing Day. I think it was when Suhabanja Village Green saw a very fierce match between Officers and Sergeants of the 10th. Names of officers and men over 45 years of age are being collected. Do not know what for. We move back still further towards the end of this week. Our bombing team were successful in a Brigade competition last week and will represent Brigade at Divisional contests.

22 Aug. Kirec, in Corps Reserve. I am fortunate in that my Brigade is going off to see yet another piece of front, the most charming part of the lot. It is life in the Highlands, almost Switzerland or Mount Troödos, pine trees and mountain paths. We shall be four days, or rather nights, on the move there, and taking over. The Italians long ago held that bit. I am getting to know the country pretty well, only the two flanks now to be visited, and I have been very near the Gulf of Orfano.

30 Aug. Krusa Balkan or Snevce front, east of Lake Doiran. There are hundreds of tortoises about; last year numbers were being sent home in tobacco tins by the troops, but it is forbidden now. We have moved to what must be the most charming scenery of any battle front, Italian included; mountainous country. It takes three hours to get from Battalion H.Q. to one Company—through beech trees and low oak scrub. In different ways it reminds one of Scotland, Norway, Cyprus and what Switzerland must be like in the summer: terrific hill-climbing to visit anyone, one hundred steps from my hut to the Mess, but it is worth it. Yesterday I had to go on duty to the regiment on our left. An hour's ride round bridle paths, cut out of the sides of mountains. The Italians have left wonderful roads and good huts. It is a real health resort; Battalion H.Q. is quite away from mosquitoes, though our outpost line still get them blown up from the valley. How long they will leave us here we do not know, but possibly two months. Wonderful views over Lake Doiran on our left where one can see through a telescope right behind the Bulgar strongholds on the " P " ridge, where the heavy fighting in April took place. I shall not forget my first view of the lake as I rode over the mountains; on a clear day one can see to the Struma as well. Only patrol encounters; neither side can do anything else. The Belashitza Mountains tower in front of us.

2 Sept. An account of the Great Fire has appeared in the home papers. It is the fourteenth fire that has visited the city; the last one was in 1910. I have not been down to see the scene, but from what I hear all the important part of the town is wiped out, including Hotel Splendide, which has just been much improved. Monastir too I understand has been much damaged by Bulgar incendiary shells. We are in an ideal spot and likely to remain some time. We get a wonderful view of Doiran front fighting.

9 Sept. Beyond the news of the evacuation of Riga and a few deserters who have come into our lines, nothing has happened. The Bulgars attacked unsuccessfully just on our right the other night, and two officers were left in our hands; one before the war was a schoolmaster near Seres. Hicks says it is likely to be Gaza for him. He nearly got killed the other day, fell out of control in a spinning nose-dive at 1,500 and only got out of it at 400. Mawson is coming out to advise on the rebuilding of Salonika.

16 Sept. It has turned distinctly cold in the mountains. Yesterday when I went out on a reconnaissance of the old Italian lines I found a rather nice dishful of tomatoes. Blackberries and figs still abound as well as grapes, so you can imagine we are not doing so badly. We are turning our minds to winter quarters now as there seems every possibility of our being in this part of the line for several months. I like what Balfour said in the House about the Balkans. An offensive on a large scale here is impossible, particularly with the number of troops we have, but I imagine we are holding most of the Bulgar army on our front and we certainly do not give them an entirely peaceful existence. More deserters have handed themselves up this week; they come in in two's and three's pretty regularly. Much interesting information is got from them. One who came in yesterday was a particularly bright lad of about 18. He had many books and maps on him and a short rifle of the very latest pattern and many bombs. I am able to procure a very liberal allowance of canteen stores for the men, and that is supplemented by fairly frequent issues of what passes as beer.

19 Sept. I was down at Corps on Monday and came back with an interpreter and deserter. The latter gave us much useful information, and yesterday we carried out a successful raid on several villages. I met several more Wykehamists at Corps. It was a committee meeting to discuss supplies, canteen stores and beer for the troops. Hicks is at Alexandria again and has visited our old haunts and friends.

26 Sept. The tray came from Beklik Mah, a village not far from Lake Tahinos. Rumours still go round that we shall leave the country, but as it would probably mean Gaza or Mesopotamia I am just as content to stay here.

10 Oct. The enemy wireless of 7/10/17 is instructive. German communiqué says, " East of Doiran an attack by a British battalion was repulsed by Bulgarian covering parties." Bulgarian official communiqué says, " An enemy battalion which advanced east of Lake Doiran was obliged to return by fire." We had a small affair on Saturday. It was a " drive " through some villages. Two small portions of two battalions were engaged, 12th Hampshires and 7th Wiltshire Regiment, and we got quite successfully to our point beyond the villages, Karali and Bulamac, without alarming enemy outposts, and then drove back to our own lines ; " repulsed " therefore is correct from their point of view ; " obliged to return by fire " is far from accurate, for they did not discover our presence till the business was just about over. Our aeroplanes were splendid and kept down their artillery fire magnificently. The guiding by night through a difficult country was very well carried out, and the fact that none of their outposts heard us till we got out speaks well for the quietness of the men. The following night the Bulgars were much alarmed, and two of their own patrols fought it out. I have just ordered 900 lbs. of turkey from the canteen. The 10th Division are now in Egypt at the back of their new front. Perhaps we shall follow when the Greeks are ready. It is said they will have an army of 350,000 in three months' time. Most of us would be glad of a change, though I like the Balkans. The hills up here are very lovely, though the pack-mules and their drivers who do all the transport would emphatically disagree with me.

14 Oct. The authorities are asking for the names of people who have not had leave since May 1916. We have just finished two deluging thunderstorms lasting many hours, just when two Companies were on the move ; however, the sun is out again. Most of the men are still under bivouacs. We shall probably remain hereabouts over Christmas, so far as we know. The views over the lake are wonderful, and some days one can see right down to where the Rupel Pass disappears into the hills.

17 Oct. The *Orient Weekly* comes out on Sundays, on other days *The Balkan News*. I see the War Office actually published a special communiqué on our recent raid. Our line at present is a very long one, and involves the best part of a day riding round it—an hour's ride from H.Q. to one Company.

21 Oct. Salonika is now a heap of cinders, and no one wants to visit it except on duty. English leave now means three clear weeks in England apart from the journey to and fro.

24 Oct. Flowers of the crocus family and cyclamens are still about in abundance, though winter is fast coming down on us. Torrential rains for two days, and the mountain paths are running streams. However, wood is very plentiful, and one can easily get everything dried. The 10th are still on the same front, but forward again in the winter line. I for one shall be sorry to leave here, though from the point of view of the Battalion we should be better off on a part of the front where there are more adequate winter quarters.

28 Oct. I expect to go off for a few days to-morrow and reconnoitre a back line which no one knows anything about. The Transport Officer and myself will take out horses and mules for forage and kit and our own food and picnic out. Incidentally as well as seeing the line we hope to get some birds which will add to our larder. It will take a day getting there and another getting back, and according as we find necessary we shall take one or two days doing the line. Soon we shall be going away from this delectable spot into reserve for a fortnight and then possibly back again into another part of the front. An Intelligence Officer friend of mine at Corps H.Q. has just lent me a very interesting book on the fighting which took place over this part of the country between the Bulgar and Greek in last Balkan War (June 30—July 31, 1913), by a Frenchman and approved by War Office, so most of the facts one can take as fairly accurate. The Greek official account is very untrustworthy.

I see another despatch is coming out about this front. I wonder if it will give any surprises. It will be instructive to see what is said of the fighting last April.

4 Nov. Sal Grec Avancé. I had a very pleasant and instructive two days and nights in some retired lines, and lived mostly on mushrooms and hares. My companion had a blunderbuss with which he did great execution. Hicks' nose-dive was into a ploughed field. The machine was smashed up, but he not at all. The first thing that arrived was an ambulance, the second a man with a camera. We are moving shortly, but not very far away. They have had two good little shows on the Struma lately. My old Brigade did them. It is just possible I may go back there.

11 Nov. We have moved into reserve camp and are moderately comfortable. The men will get some chance of football, sports and boxing. I am having a platoon football competition throughout the battalion.

19 Nov. The mountains opposite, the Belashitza or Beles Range, are now capped with snow, and we had a severe frost last night. The third blanket has been served to all ranks, so although we are in tents and bivouacs whilst in reserve we are managing to keep warm. As a matter of fact the men are much healthier this weather with no more mosquitoes. The nets are withdrawn, and whale oil issued in their place. We go into the line again on Saturday. Meanwhile in addition to work on roads and range firing, we are having football leagues and battalion sports. We are winding up our out-of-the-line period with a third and last concert at the Y.M.C.A. on Wednesday evening. It is very jolly getting the battalion together for once in a way ; it then becomes practicable to do something for them regimentally : at other times any amusement must be run by the Company, and judging from most of the letters the men get horribly fed up with the monotony night after night on sentry or outpost duty, especially when we are below strength, as we usually are during the summer months owing to malaria. I am beginning to feel I could do with a bit of leave, but it is off again, owing to affairs in Italy I fancy ; at any rate the last leave party got as far as Old Greece, and then were sent back to their battalions.

25 Nov. Popovo. We moved yesterday from reserve into the left sector of our front, where we get a view of much liveliness, though our bit is quiet enough. Powell has taken over command of A Company on the right of our Battalion line. Our fortnight in reserve was quite a good time. The sports last Tuesday were quite a success, and the General honoured us with his presence. There is a lot of air activity just at present on this front both from our 'planes and the enemy's. Hicks has gone to the Palestine front. We are making charcoal for the winter. My old Brigade have moved down to extreme right of line, on the Gulf of Orfano.

29 Nov. The French have taken over our late part of the line east of the Vardar ; the Bulgars announce in their communiqué that they have taken prisoners " some black Frenchmen," so when we leave here it will either be Doiran or Struma front if we are to remain in the country. It is wonderful weather for November, and quite hot again. I get about seven hours walking up hill and down dale, and am quite ready for bed by the time evening comes. I expect to have a show of my own shortly somewhere on this front, artillery and some two companies or more. The cheese ration has started again, which is a great joy to all. Leave still gets held up periodically.

9 Dec. The six platoons I took out yesterday to Bulamac did quite well, and we occupied and held for the allotted time our three villages : left our line at 4.20 a.m. and got back about 10 a.m. Only had one man touched, though they gave us a pretty good shelling coming home. The men came back over the plain in excellent form, little groups well closed up, in fact orders could not have been carried out better. Though we had no great difficulties to encounter, yet a night show is always ticklish work, especially as we had a small river to cross. The cold was intense, and of course we got pretty wet getting over. The Bulgar post cleared from the village a few moments before we sighted it. One gentleman had been reading a Turkish newspaper on a straw bed before extinguishing his light and departing.

16 Dec. We shall stay here I think, which is good news. A very valuable deserter surrendered to us on Friday, a Greek of Bogdanci, and we learned much of him with the help of bully beef and cigarettes ; he talked much.

19 Dec. We got four prisoners yesterday, and incidentally some valuable information. The party, twenty-five of No. 15 Platoon, rushed them silently and no shot was fired on either side. Willis, the Intelligence Officer, put his revolver in one man's stomach and said " finish Johnny." He agreed, put up his hands and said in good American, " Don't be frightened : only four of us."

23 Dec. Although we shall be in the line for Christmas Day, I do not think the men will have such a bad time. Have distributed an enormous quantity of canteen stores, and every man has a present from Queen Alexandra's Field Force Fund. In addition there is beer, and every N.C.O. gets a bottle of stout. Plum puddings, which are not provided free by Government this year, are being paid for by the officers, and everyone should get a bite of turkey (twenty-five men to a bird). I have not seen the birds yet ; that is the last thing to draw, and transport will be doing that to-morrow. To-morrow H.Q. Officers shoot against the N.C.O.'s with the Bulgar rifles brought in by our patrol the other day. The Corps Commander was round on Friday and congratulated the Colonel on success of patrol. On Christmas Day the transport are having sports and mule races, and a minor Horse Show. In the evening the reserve Company are having a concert. The Adjutant went off with scarlet fever yesterday, so we are wondering if we shall be isolated and remain here for the rest of the war. It is not a bad place to take up a permanent abode in.

26 Dec. Christmas Day is over and everything passed off quite well. Turkeys and plum puddings turned up, and from the considerable balance we have in Regimental funds we were able to make a free issue of both.

30 Dec. Hicks is back on the Gaza front with his R.F.C. Squadron. He wants me to do Cairo and Luxor with him soon. I may put in for Egyptian leave shortly. If I do it at all I must do it soon, before the really hot weather comes on. Willis, our Intelligence Officer, has just got the M.C. for his good work in taking prisoners the other day.

1918.

3 Jan. I have written two historical things on the last two Balkan Wars for the *Balkan News*. They will be of interest to a few out here, and are the result of reading and personal enquiries and exploration.

5 Jan. Snow is thick around us. It is bitterly cold, even at H.Q., and the men in the trenches are still worse off. The Colonel and I went down to dinner with a Balloon Section, and saw a cinema show last night. It was quite entertaining. The men will see it when we get back into reserve next week. The mud could not be worse, though the frost has temporarily hardened up the ground. The Vardar wind is starting too. Though I have a nice wood fire in my shack, the wind is always inside, and the only warm place is under the blankets.

23 Jan. New C.O., Lieut.-Colonel G. S. McNaught of the Cheshire Regiment, has arrived.

10 Feb. Dova Tepe Sector. I was away last week from Monday to Thursday. We had a very enjoyable Old Wykehamist Dinner on Tuesday, 5 Feb.; about forty present. We stayed at the new Officers' Rest House, which is a very comfortable place, and met several people I had not seen or heard of for years. It is very misty and chilly to-day, so the C.O. and I are going to take the opportunity this afternoon of looking round our line and looking at it from in front. The Bulgar is too watchful on fine and clear days, and takes advantage of any target he can get for his guns. We are still on the same front, and as yet no signs of a move. It was the first time I had seen Salonika since the fire. There can have been few fires that have done so much damage. We were fortunate in getting a friend in the Mechanical Transport to motor us back the whole way.

21 Feb. Very bad news from the 10th Battalion. Faith wrote me a few days ago saying Colonel Beckett had been accidentally killed in a bomb accident on Saturday, 9 Feb. He was returning with a Battery Commander and the Regimental M.O. from visiting his day posts, and on the way back to H.Q. passed his bombing officer taking a class of N.C.O.'s. He saw a corporal throw a bomb and then got down into the trench beside him and told him to throw his last. The corporal did so, but the bomb exploded on leaving his hand. The corporal was wounded in the hand, the bombing officer in the leg. Colonel Beckett got a section in his head and another bit through his right shoulder. He became unconscious at once, and died in three or four minutes. The other two officers near by were untouched. He was buried in a British cemetery in the Battalion lines, just over the Struma. He was one of the best, and had been through it since Le Cateau. D.S.O., Brevet Lieut.-Colonel, Serbian White Eagle, and might have got a Brigade any time. He was thought an enormous lot of in the Division, and had made the 10th Hampshires into a very fine Battalion.

5 May. Friday I motored to Salonika and back to inspect Army Training School. All the flags were flying half-mast on Greek buildings and vessels, and bells tolling. It turned out to be the Greek Good Friday. We are still in Corps Reserve near Kirec, digging most of the time.

18 Sept. Attack on White Scar Hill, in conjunction with main attack on " P " ridge. The Battalion (that part of it which was in it) distinguished itself yesterday. We had to demonstrate against, attack, and hold a hill for a stated period, a small part of larger operations. We did it twice and got blown off twice by, it seemed, every gun in Macedonia. I ran the second half of operations. We drove off a Bulgar counter-attack and all wires being cut by shell-fire eventually a runner got through to me that the General ordered us to withdraw as we had done all that was wanted. I think we got all the wounded away ; the company killed a good few Bulgars, including an officer ; I have got some wonderful souvenirs which I found in his dug-out. Last night came through congratulations to the Battalion from the Divisional Commander. Everything is going on excellently. A Company was raided last night, but the Bulgar was driven off and did not get into our trenches ; that was one excitement during the night ; and shortly after that was over we were shelled with gas-shells, our first experience, but no damage done.

27 Sept. Everything has gone splendidly. The offensive opened on 18th, only nine days ago, and here I am sitting in a field outside Strumnitza in Bulgaria. Everyone was very pleased with the work the Battalion did on the 18th. Ours was only a small part of very big operations, but it was eminently successful. The first really successful show I have taken part in, and all went like clockwork. Then followed what must have been the Bulgars' despairing effort on A Company. Since 18th it has been march, march, march. The men have marched well in spite of terrific heat and dust. One is at last really proud to be in the British Army in Macedonia. A car passed us yesterday, two Bulgar colonels who were surrendering, and a representative of Government on their way to G.H.Q. to try to fix terms. Ready for unconditional surrender to British and French, but in terror of Greeks and Serbs. The former are being kept well in hand by us so far. They too have fought well. Our Brigade was first into Bulgaria, and has done very well throughout. This is ever so much better than the stationary life we were living, and the men are in the highest spirits. I do not yet know our next move. I would not have missed any of this for the world.

1 Oct. Our war was brought to a successful conclusion yesterday at 12 midday when hostilities ceased. The offensive started with terrific attacks (gas and everything) on September 18. Since then we have been following up the Bulgar ceaselessly and were climbing mountains all the night of 29th/30th, and when we got to the top had orders to come to the bottom again, and then learned that the Bulgar had surrendered unconditionally. The marching we have done lately has been terrific, and now it is over, and we are resting and refitting, and tonight I shall be in pyjamas again under the shade of a tree, washed, shaved, and in my right mind. The men are fagged out but jubilant, and naturally after close on three years of varying monotony. The Bulgar put up a very determined resistance, and the material we have taken must be very large. Just in our little bit I have seen all kinds from heavy guns to the meanest souvenirs. We also got gassed on 19th, though not badly. The Brigade has done splendidly, and I think we were the first into Bulgaria. We entered by the Kosturino Pass, and were on our way to the Upper Struma to cut off the Bulgar Struma forces when surrender came. I do not know the next move. I hope we may go to Sofia. Some of our men and the Bulgar wounded whom we found in their hospitals were in a fearful condition.

7 Oct. Our division has been selected from the Allied Armies for Army of Occupation in Bulgaria. One has seen something, and heard more of the unpleasant side of war—I mean the occupation of enemy country. It is just as well the Greek and Serb is being rigorously kept out of Bulgaria, for the peasants we are now meeting are delightful and quite inoffensive farmers, and have done nothing to merit the treatment the Serbs and Greeks would like to give them.

12 Oct. Having got nearly half the way to Sofia, my orders came to report at the " Infantry Base Depot, Salonika." I fancy I shall have Indian troops to look after there, and that we may return up country with them some time. It is a disappointment only to have gone halfway to Sofia with the Battalion.

13 Oct. Am still at wayside station hoping to get on down the line some day. Numerous adventures trying to get hold of our kit, which is going up the line, whilst we are going down. The railway line is still run by Bulgars, who are most friendly ; one washed up my breakfast things this morning, in return for remains of my bully beef. I wish I knew a word of German, as no one seems to know French, which causes perpetual difficulties.

14 Oct. I arrived at Strumnitza last night after picking up some of my kit. I am staying here to-night so as to see my canteen sergeant who is on his way up the line ; then on to Doiran and the base. A

Bulgar (? Macedonian) lad (bandsman, aged 17) just demobilized has been doing servant to me. This morning I lunched with his family in the town. Strumnitza is a pretty place. I like Macedonia more and more, but long for leave. From the scanty news we get, it looks very hopeful. People here talk about the war ending this year. The Bulgar is a clean fighter. We are all at peace here now : what is going to happen to us next I do not know. I shall be near the Base for a time, I suppose, but I do not anticipate much difficulty in getting leave now, though I am sorry to leave the Battalion.

APPENDIX I.

26TH DIVISIONAL ORDER, DATED 19 SEPT., 1918 :—

The Divisional Commander wishes to express his appreciation of the gallant behaviour of the 8th D.C.L.I. and 12th Hampshires during the day's operations, and regrets to hear that their casualties were so heavy.

Their attack was carried out with success, and in spite of very intense shell-fire they held the ground gained with great tenacity and determination until ordered to withdraw.

APPENDIX II.

NOTES MADE DURING ADVANCE INTO BULGARIA.

Wed., 18 Sept. 1918. British offensive opens, 5 a.m. Attack on " P " ridge. 12th Hampshires attack and take White Scar Hill (part of which is in Serbia). 8th D.C.L.I. attack Flat Iron Hill.

18/19 Sept. Raid of a Bulgar battalion on Glengarry Hill driven off by A Company, 12th Hampshires. Second attack on " P " ridge. Turning movement by Serbs, French and Greeks develops.

Sat., 21 Sept. General Bulgar retirement. Orders to us to concentrate in evening. Our patrols report Boyau westwards evacuated by enemy. Dumps being blown up behind enemy lines. Gevghelli in flames.

Sun., 22 Sept. We move forward and concentrate in area Helmet Hill - Little Bekirli at 4 a.m.

10 a.m. pass the boundary stone and enter Serbia.

Ride on and pass through enemy wire to Pyramide.

Bulgar 68th Regimental Headquarters at Twin Hill become our Battalion Headquarters.

Visit from Divisional Commander (Major-General Gay), who congratulates us on White Scar battle. Land mine on our left—dumps in flames.

Mon., 23 Sept. Orders at 1 a.m. to move at 5.30 a.m. Enemy apparently holding line Paljorca - Cinarle Dere. One or two lights go up, and a barrage is registered in front of this line of heights.

First view of rear of Mitrailleuse and Bogorodica and Stojakovo. Twin Hill is a veritable fortress, and could never have been taken. Our advance is undoubtedly mainly due to Serb - French - Greek turning movements, though Anglo-Greek attacks must have held large enemy forces.

Corps move to-day from Janes to Reselli, where 26th Division now are. Greeks are on our right to-day.

Cavalry patrols came through us at dusk last evening.

Corpl. Harrison wounded and missing in Dautli fight found after being out from 18th to 22nd.

We hoped to get to White Scar to-day to bury dead, but could not. Move *via* Stojakovo to Bogdanci. Battalion moves off again 5 p.m. and takes up outpost position on hills above latter. A and D Companies in position by 8 p.m.

Tues., 24 Sept. Moved off from Schwazburg Est at 7 a.m., D Coy. advanced guard. Devons took Casandule, and we moved up on left, arriving at 11 a.m. Enemy shelling plain in front. 78th Brigade moved up on our left. At 10.30 p.m. Battalion moved down first-class military road across Boyima Valley to neighbourhood of hospital at Rabrovo. Some of our wounded found there.

Wed., 25 Sept. 8.15 a.m. Moved up Strumnitza Road to neighbourhood of Kosturino.

9.30 a.m. Kosturino taken by 8th D.C.L.I.

Hot and smelly march, very dusty. Greeks on right, 78th Brigade on left of ours (79th). 79th form Kosturino Salient.

In afternoon we are holding new line : C Company in touch with 78th Brigade, D Company in centre, A Company on right in touch with Greeks.

8th D.C.L.I. on outpost duty on hills north of Kosturino. Devons relieved by us and go into Brigade Reserve. Kits come up, and Bn. Headquarters get a night in bed.

Thurs., 26 Sept. We enter Bulgarian territory. Long day's march from Kosturino to Strumnitza. 8th D.C.L.I. and R.F.A. Brigade advanced guard, 12th Hampshires head of main guard. Very dirty and tiring march. Men marched very well, only five did not turn up at end of day. I marched in rear of Battalion all day encouraging stragglers. I found in Rabrovo Hospital as prisoners and wounded Corpl. Davis, Privates Butlin, Ashley and Jones ; they had been there two or three days, and had been taken prisoners on White Scar Hill on 18th.

Fri., 27 Sept. Patrols sent out to neighbouring villages. Everyone very fit and cheerful. Two Bulgar Colonels, representatives of Bulgar Government, passed by us in car yesterday on way to G.H.Q. to see what terms they can get. It is rumoured that they will accept anything we and the French offer, provided Greeks and Serbs are kept out of their territory.

Camp in fields outside Strumnitza. Many vegetables about.

6 p.m. We move to Cradosor, north of Strumnitza, and make perimeter camp round village. A good night.

Sat., 28 Sept. Reconnaissance of Vasiljevo and Dobrenci. Piquets of one platoon each on Radovista Road and Berovo Road by Dobrenci.

4.15 p.m. Move off *via* Vasiljevo, where man comes up with story of throat-cuttings, Dobrosinci, Jenimahale to near Canakcili at foothills.

The village of Dobrosinci come out, the headman with white flag and men with hats off to C.O. and self when we ride up. They offer salt and bread, and the women pour flowers on us and try to decorate our horses' bridles. They are " all loyal Serbs and Greeks," but some look very like ex-Bulgar soldiers.

We arrived at dark at a waterless spot.

Sun., 29 Sept.. We find water, and are ordered to move *via* Hamzali to Berovo. Heavy gun-fire in direction of Struma. Arrive at foot of road below Hamzali, where 8th D.C.L.I. are held up by accurate shelling.

All day delay, but finally D Company move again at 11.30 p.m.

Mon., 30 Sept. B and C Companies move at 2.15 a.m., A and Headquarters at 4 a.m., and climb hills (what hills !) on east of the main road to attempt turning movement.

We hear that the *War is over*, and hostilities are to cease at 12 noon with unconditional surrender.

11 a.m. Return to foot of hills, breakfast and clean up.

7.15 p.m. Battalion arrives at Dabilja. I went ahead to select camping sites.

Tues., 1 Oct. Reorganization of Battalion in two Companies, under Major Jones (No. 1) and Captain Hubback (No. 2). Day of comparative rest.

Wed., 2 Oct. At 3 p.m. orders to be prepared to move, as there is a possibility of hostilities again breaking out.

5 p.m. Meeting of C.O.'s at Brigade, where they are told British Army is to march into Bulgaria as Army of Occupation, whilst French and Serbs occupy Serbia.

Thurs., 3 Oct. Visit Prosenik with the Padré and get various supplies from the villagers.

Fri., 4 Oct. Companies getting straight and being smartened up. Transport inspection.

Sat., 5 Oct. Preparing for move " eastwards," and heavy rain.

Sun., 6 Oct. Heavy rain. River rises and outs off Brigade and Battalion Headquarters from the road we are to move on. March east along Strumica Valley. Halt for lunch at Trnvo, for night in a field near Jenikoi. Rain all day and night following. Men are without bivouacs and blankets.

Mon., 7 Oct. Remained at Jenikoi. Road ahead apparently still congested with Bulgars. News received that King Ferdinand has abdicated in favour of Prince Boris. Instructions received to cultivate friendly relations with the Bulgars.

Tues., 8 Oct. Still at Jenikoi. Decorations for other ranks for White Scar Battle come through—four Military Medals for 12th Hampshires.

Wed., 9 Oct. Marched from Jenikoi, which is 30 kilos from Petric, to a point 11 kilos from Petric. Pouring rain all day. 12th Hampshires behind Brigade Headquarters. We pass Bulgar outposts, still armed, presumably to prevent Greeks, Serbs and French entering their territory. Pass their railhead dump and camp on banks of Strumica.

Thurs., 10 Oct. A delightful camp, and many bathe in Strumica. Move off at 9.30 a.m., and rear of Battalion arrives in next camp at 1 p.m. Hot sunny afternoon: all are able to dry kit, etc. We camp by track under hills north of Strumica River in Petric - Prepecina neighbourhood, after marching about 10 kilos.

Fri., 11 Oct. Heavy dew and a delightful spot. Good water and plenty of hay.

March across Struma by Livunovo Bridge to camp by Bistritza River (17 kilos). Powell and I are ordered to report at Infantry Base Camp at Summerhill for duty with Indian Battalions. We are to find our way by Decauville and motor lorry, taking two days' rations.

Sat., 12 Oct. On this day I left the 12th Hampshires and never rejoined them.

www.ingramcontent.com/pod-product-compliance
Lightning Source LLC
Chambersburg PA
CBHW070208100426
42743CB00013B/3100